CALMING

Mandalas

AN ADULT COLORING BOOK

Vol. 6

Zhena Khasha Books

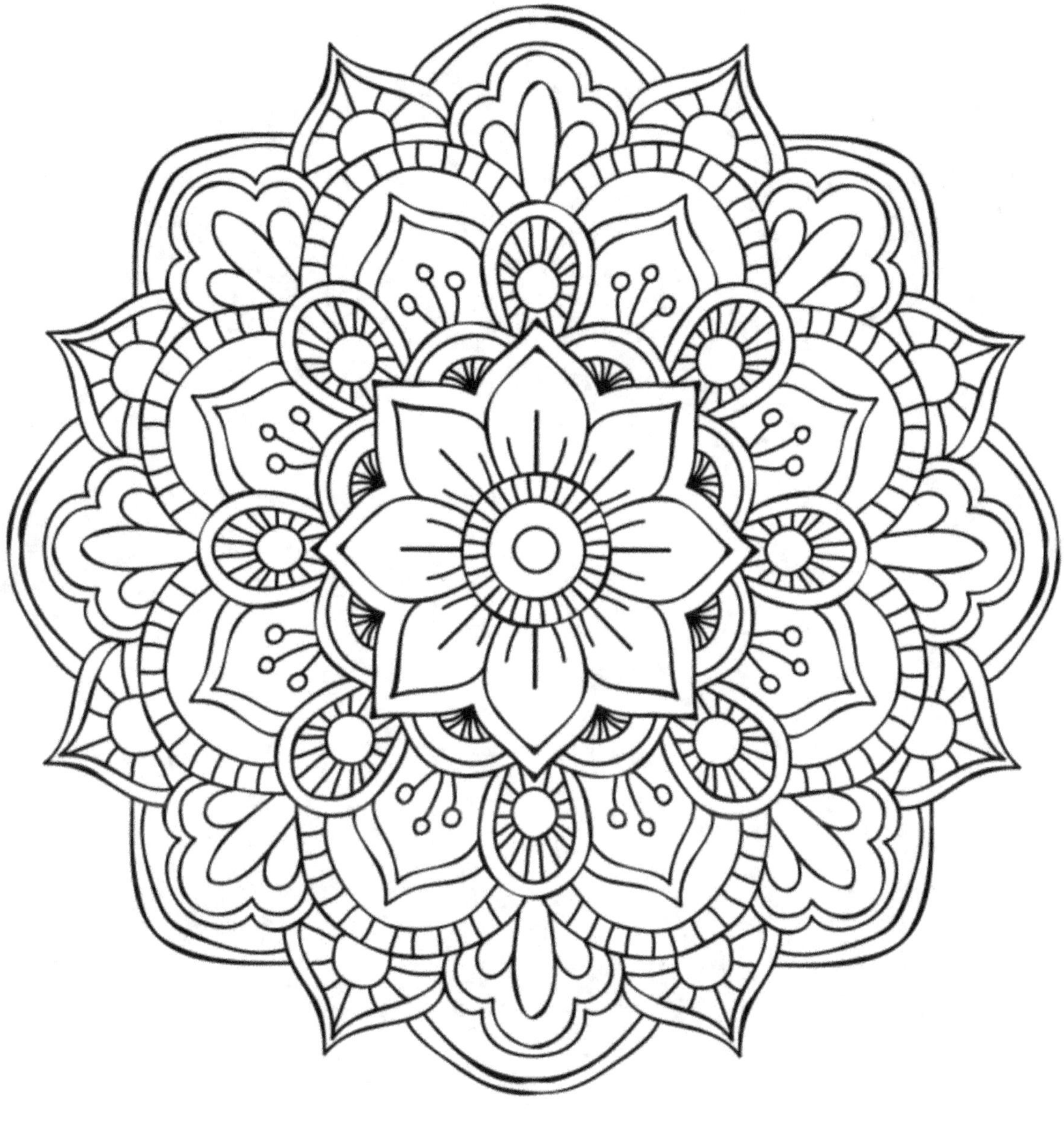

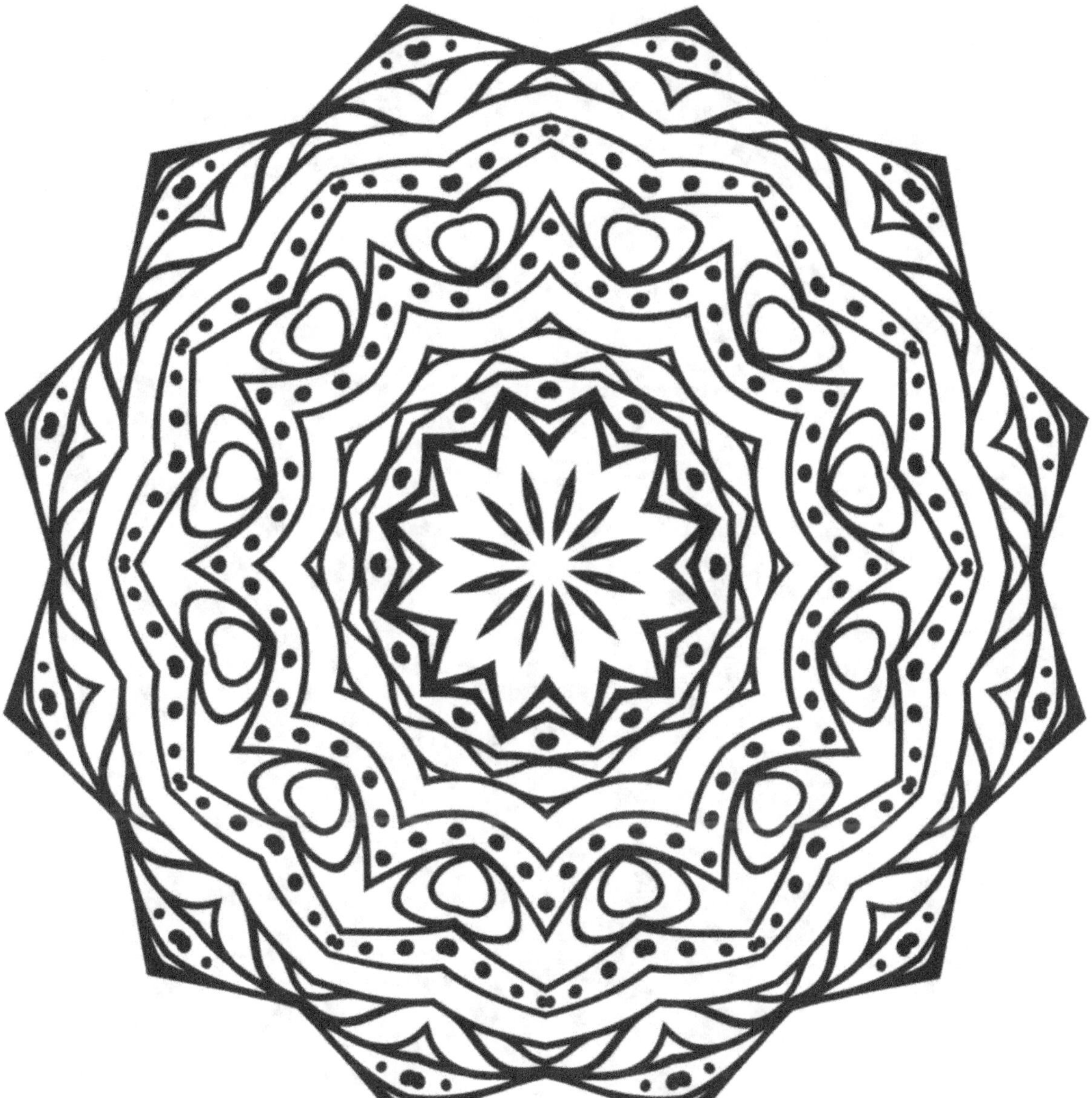

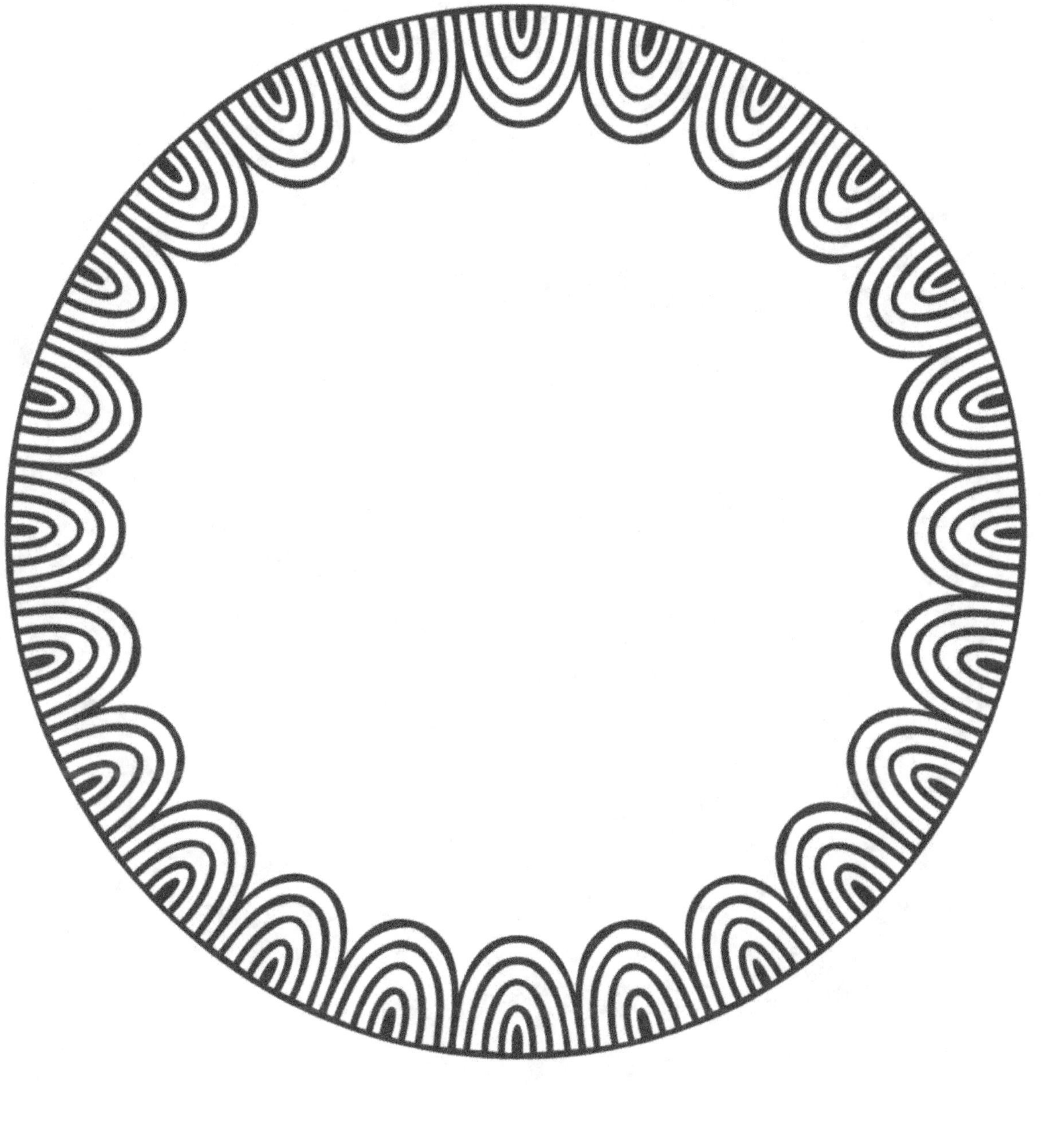

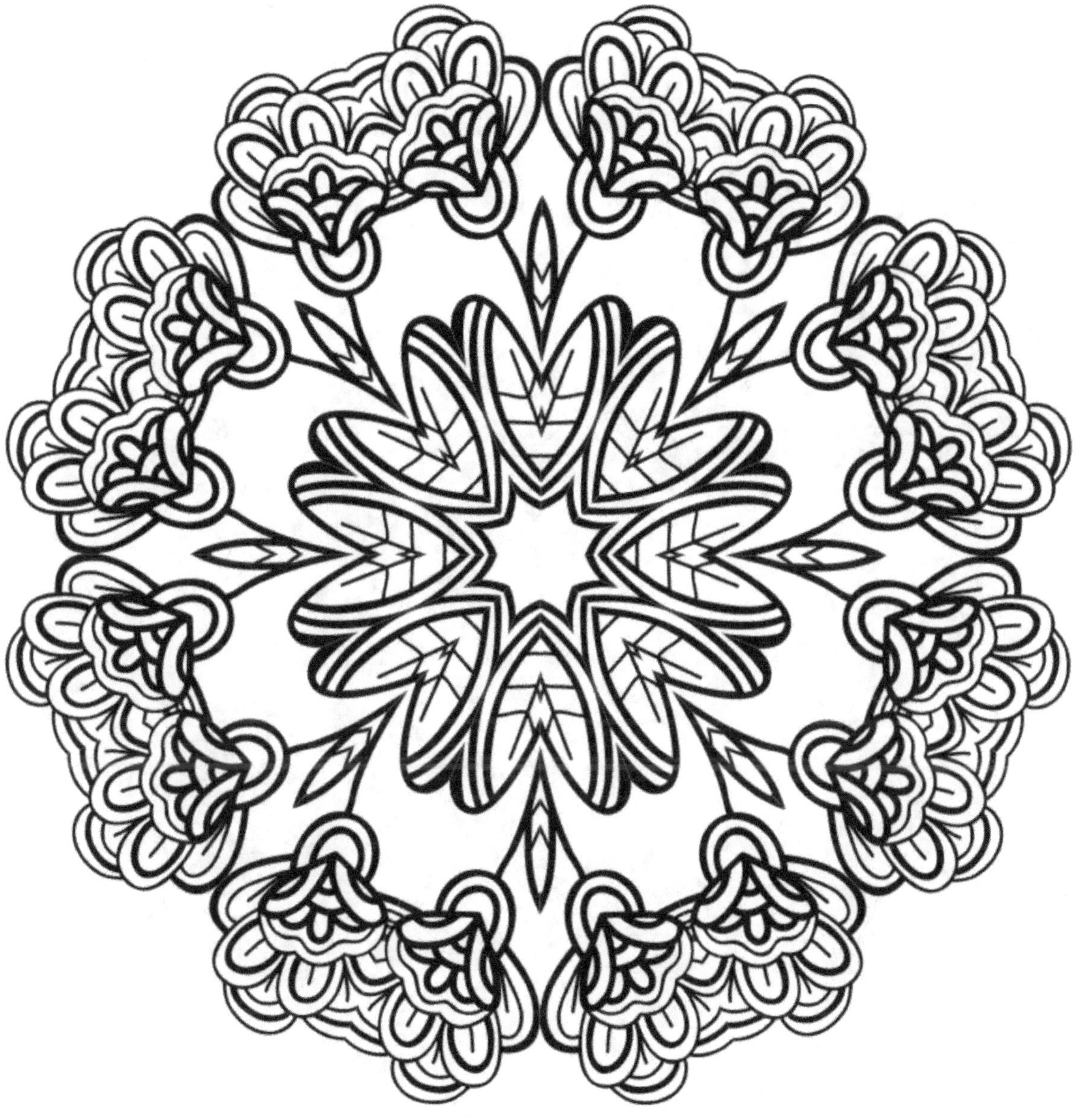

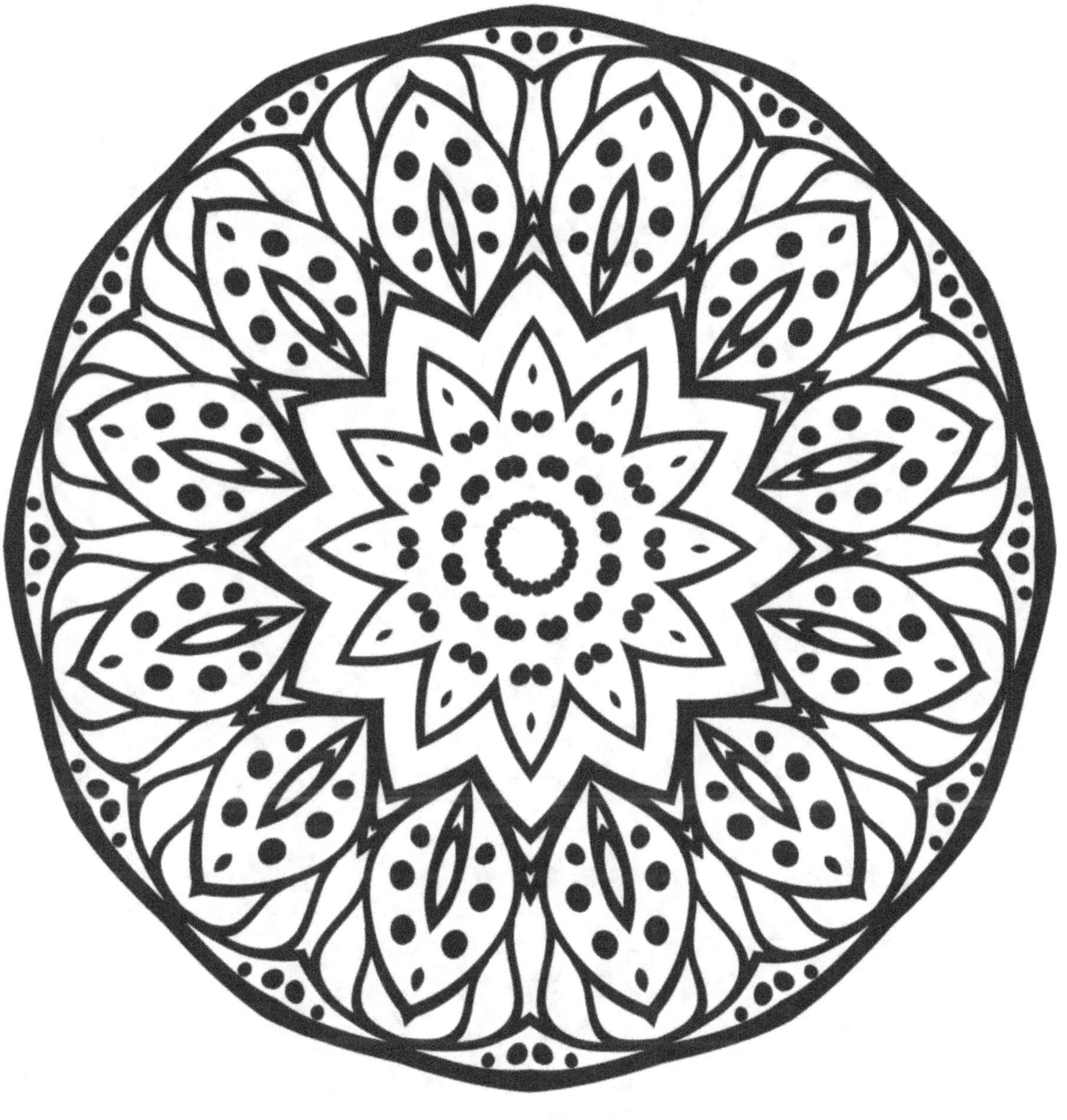

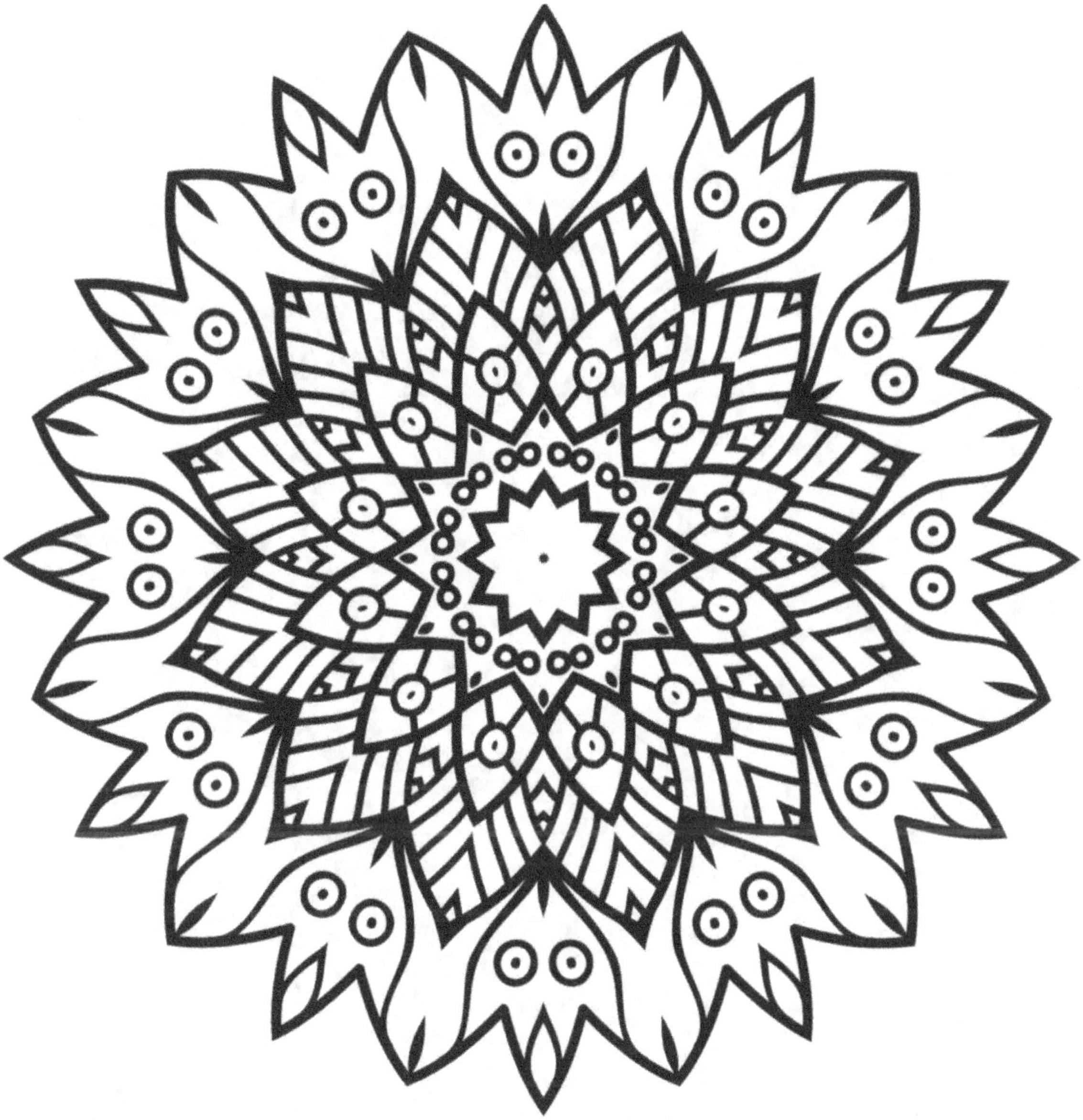

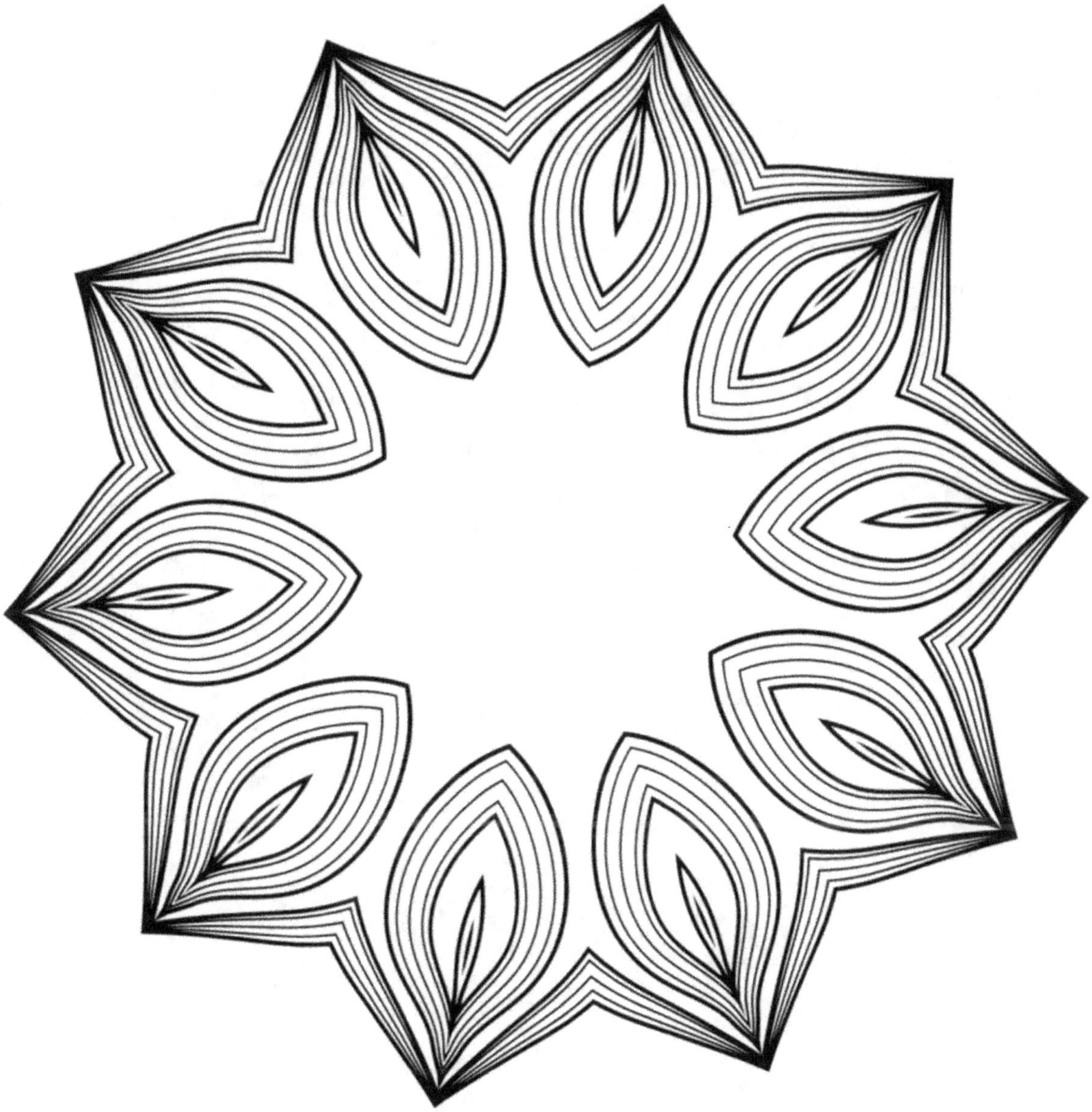

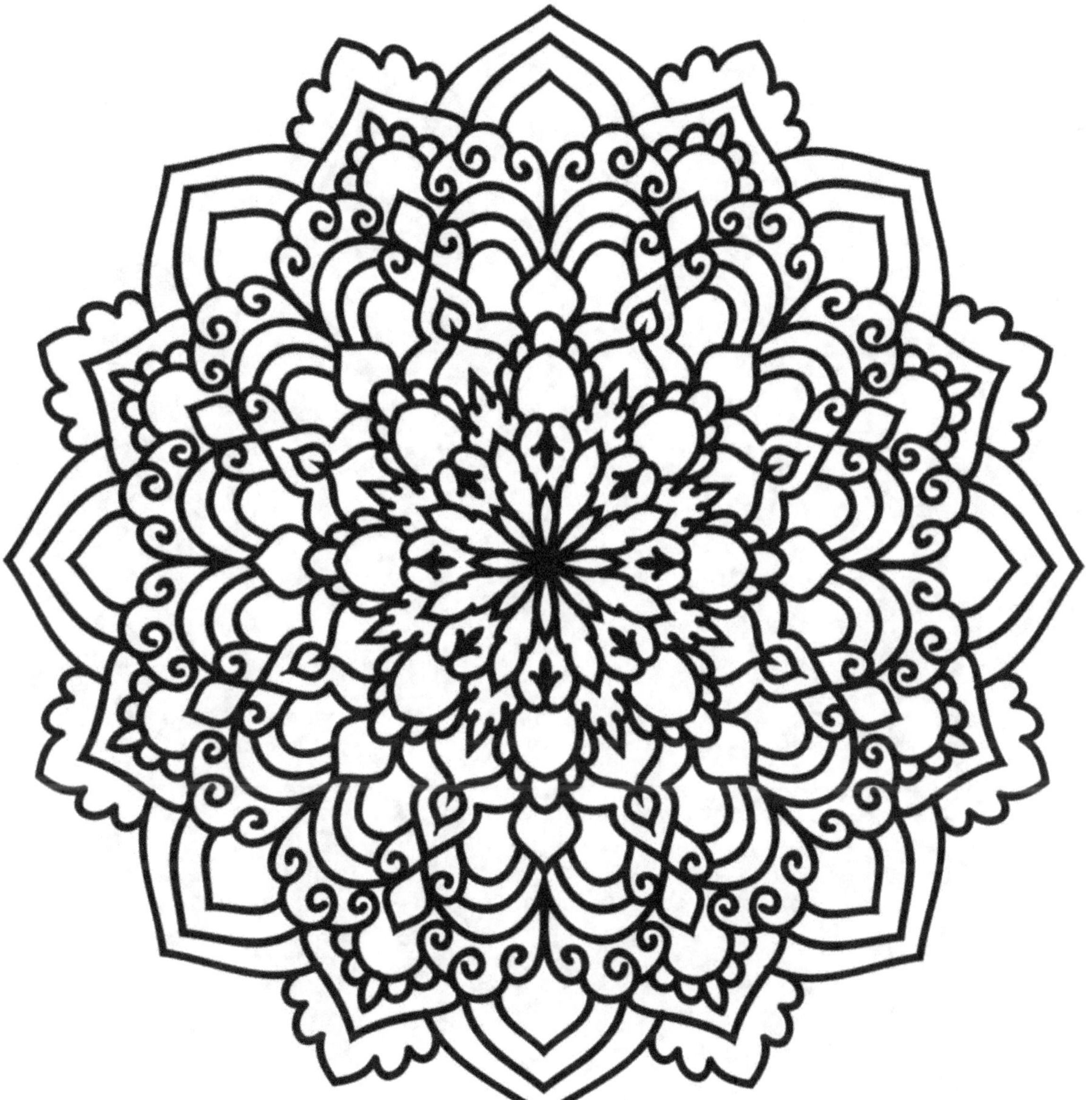

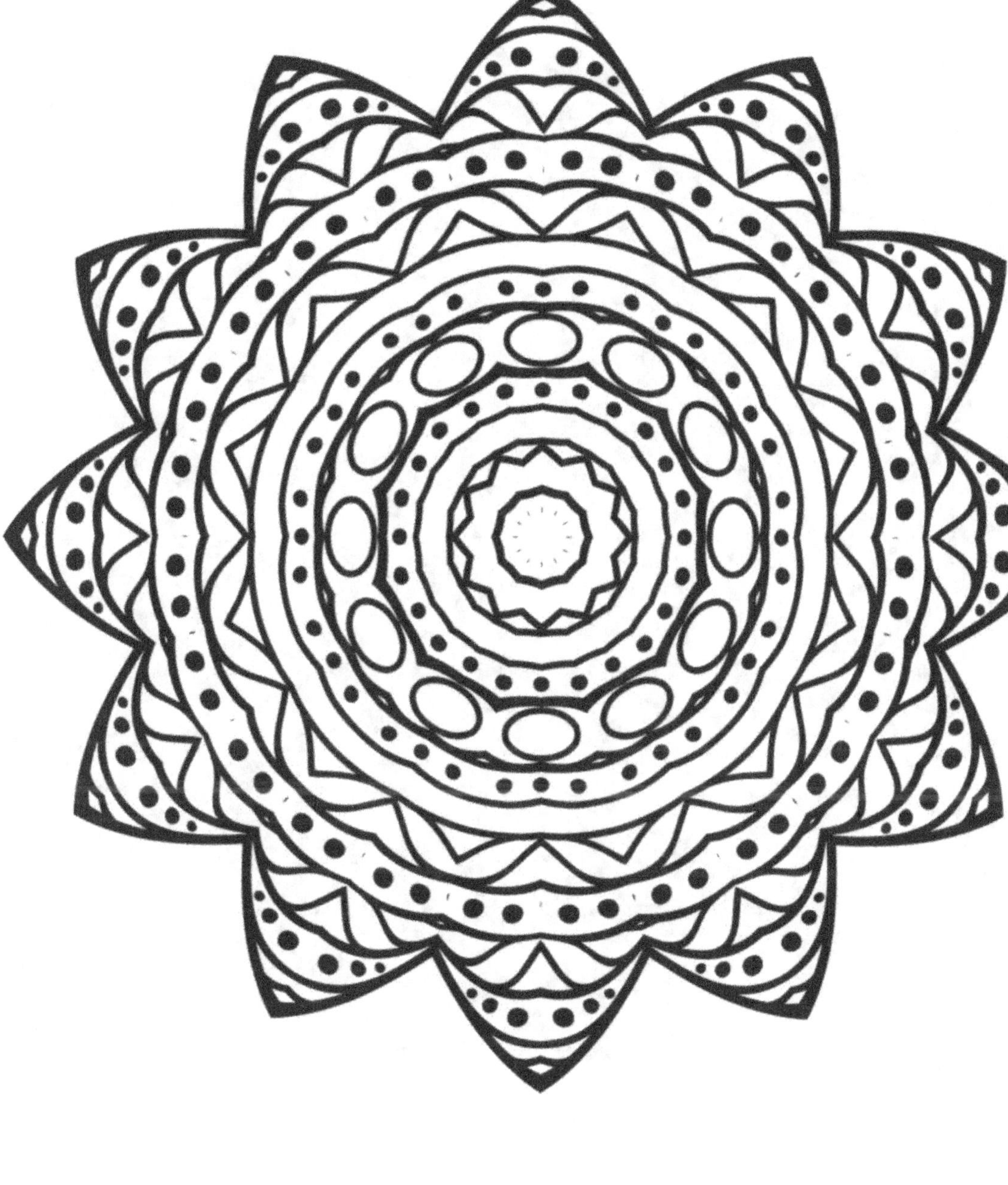

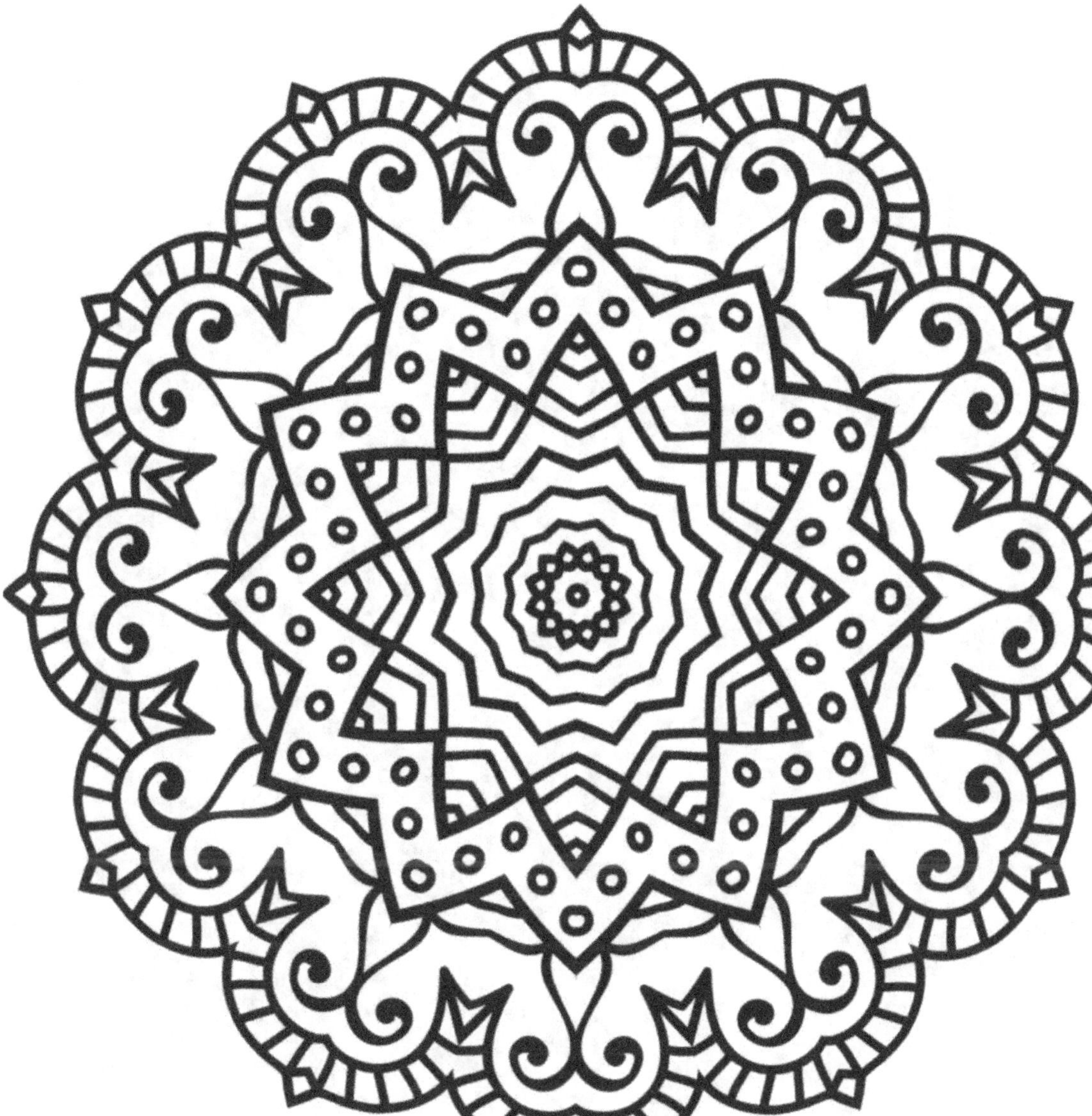

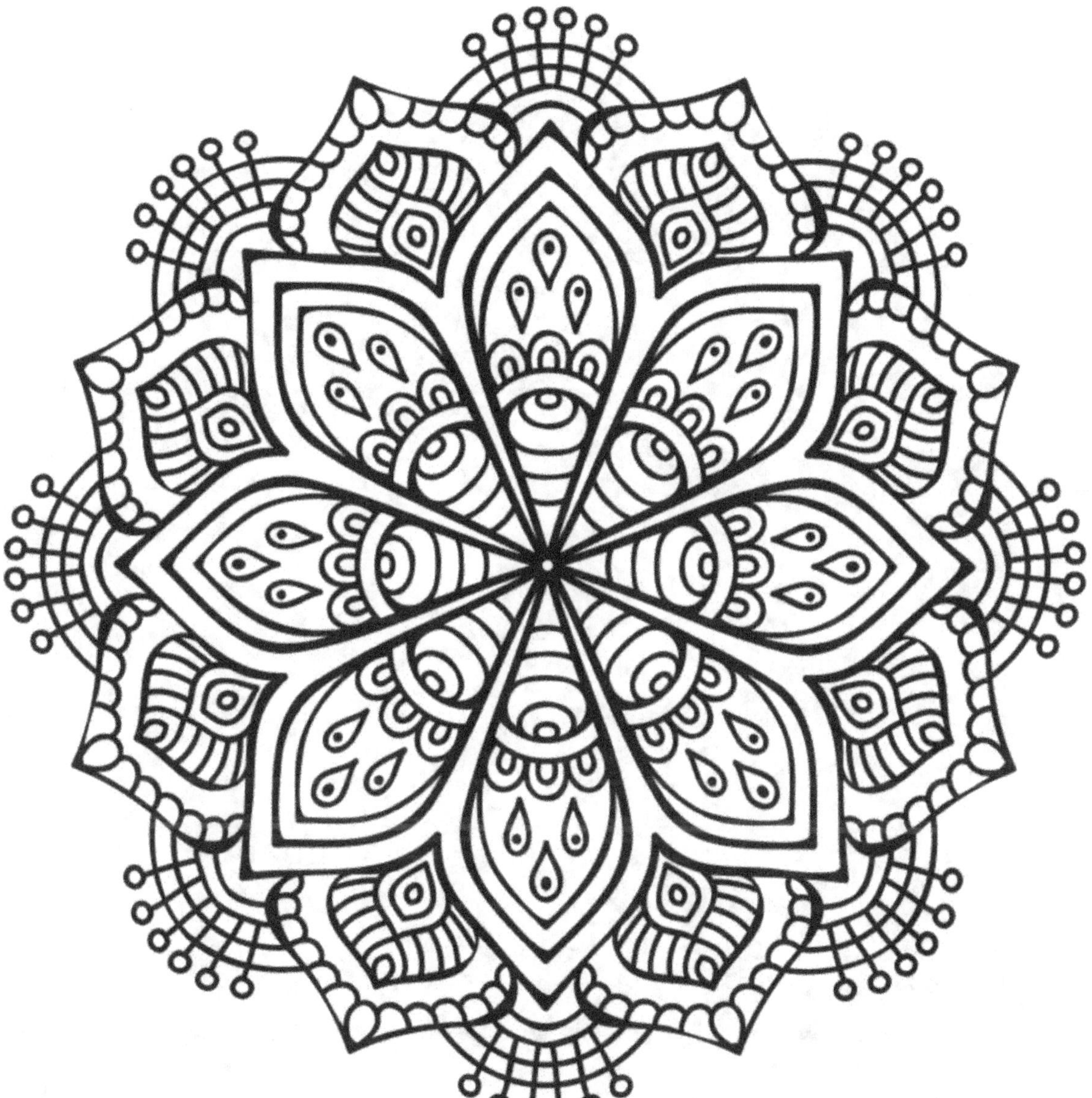

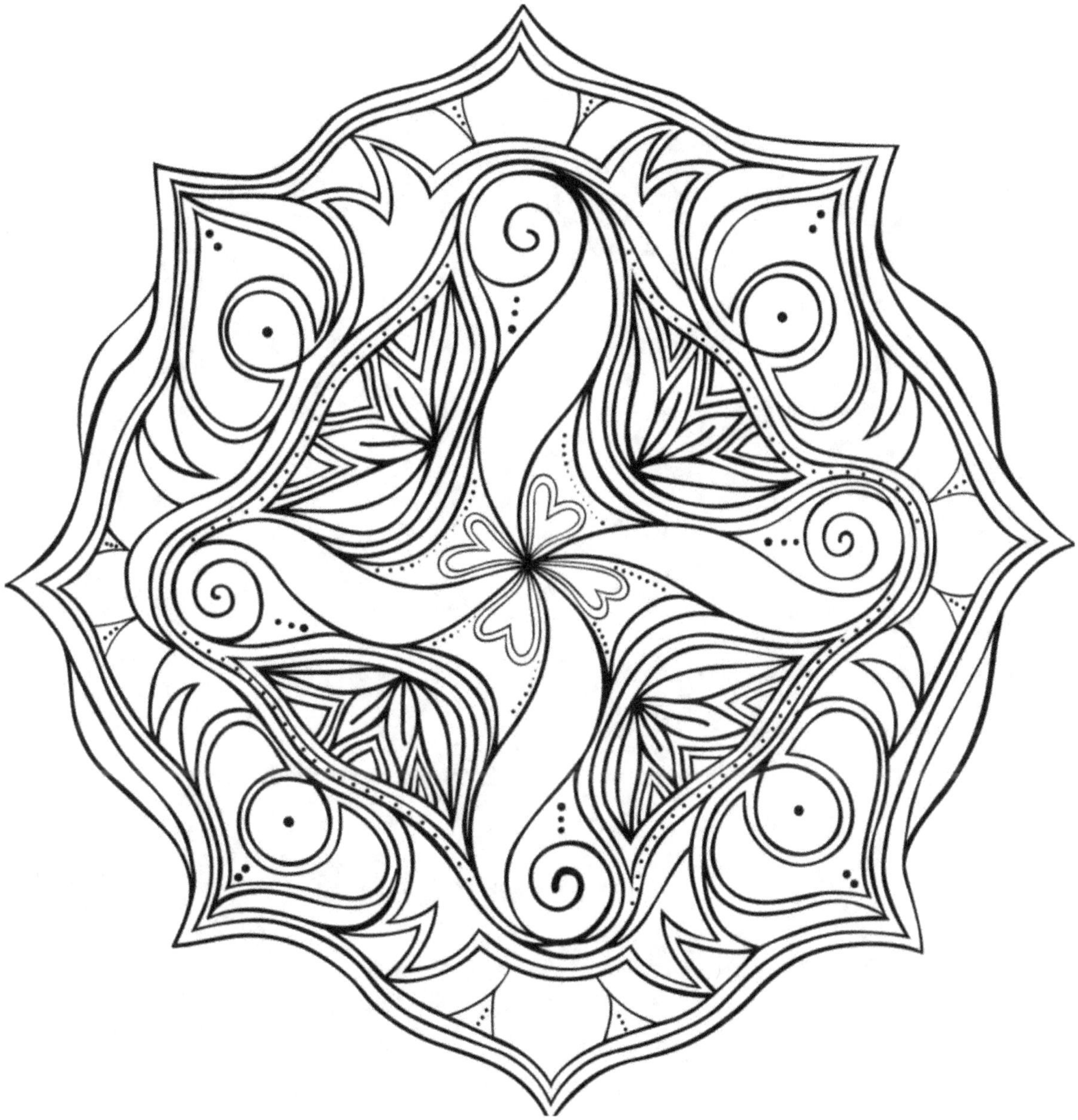

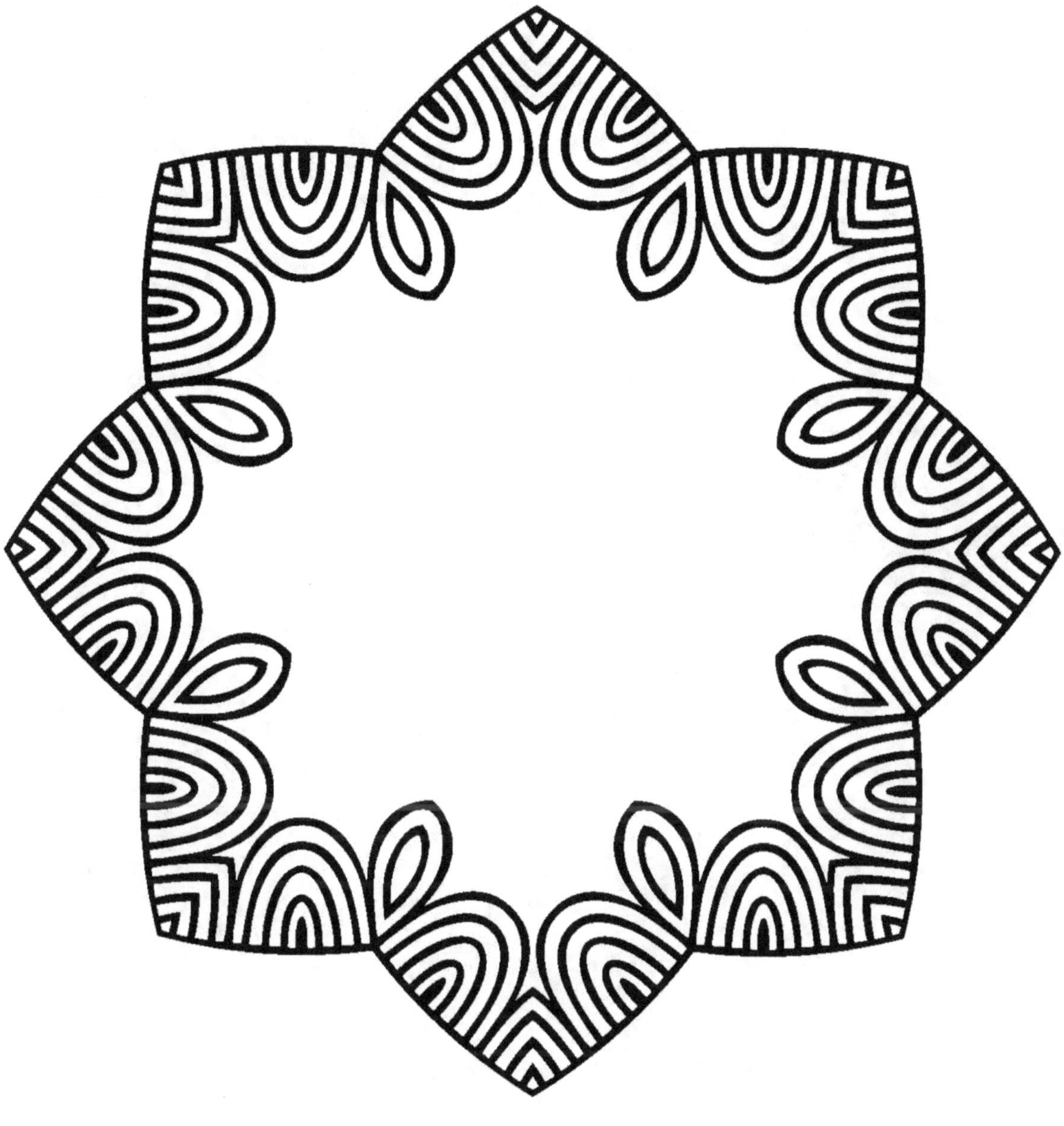

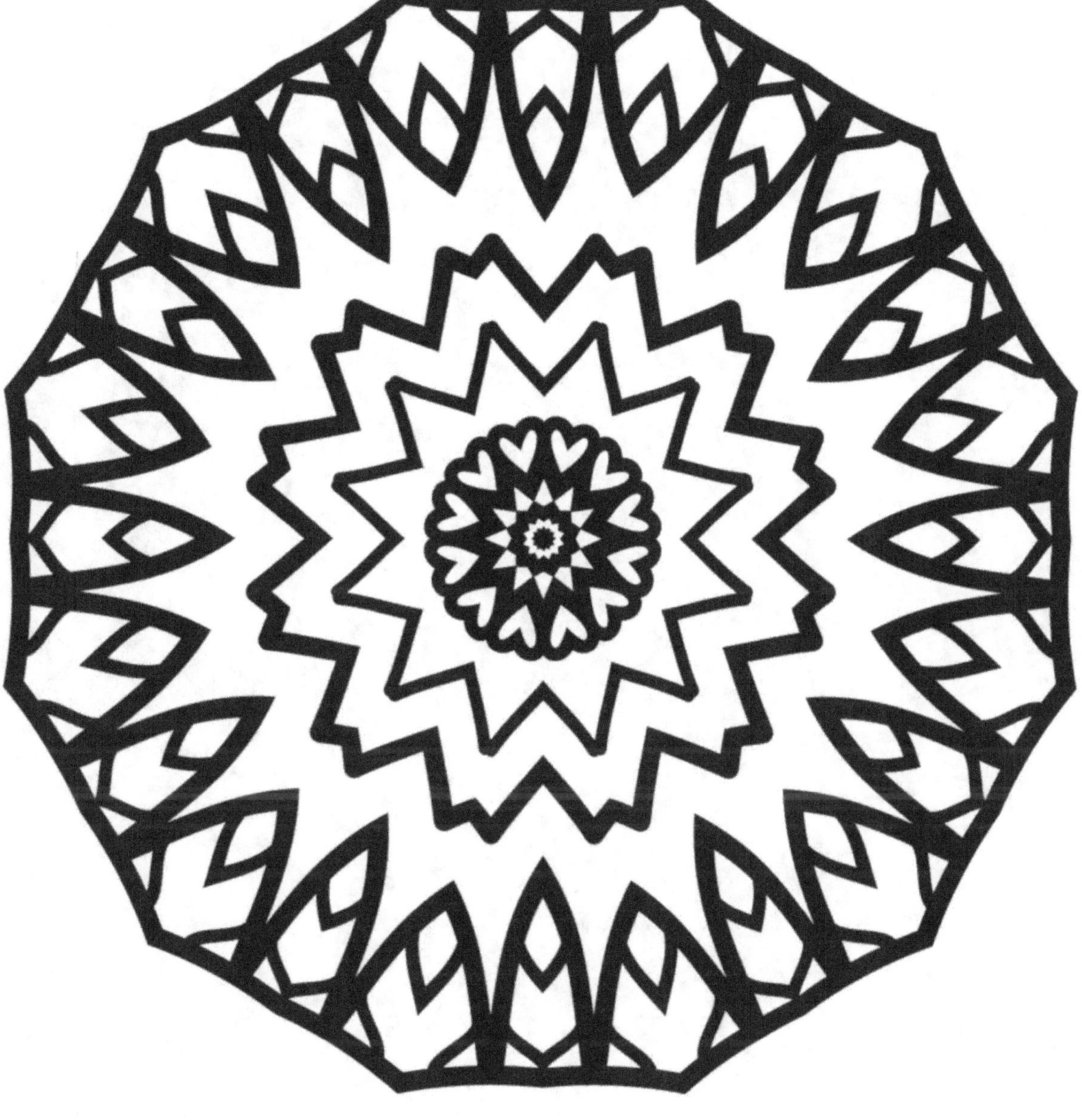

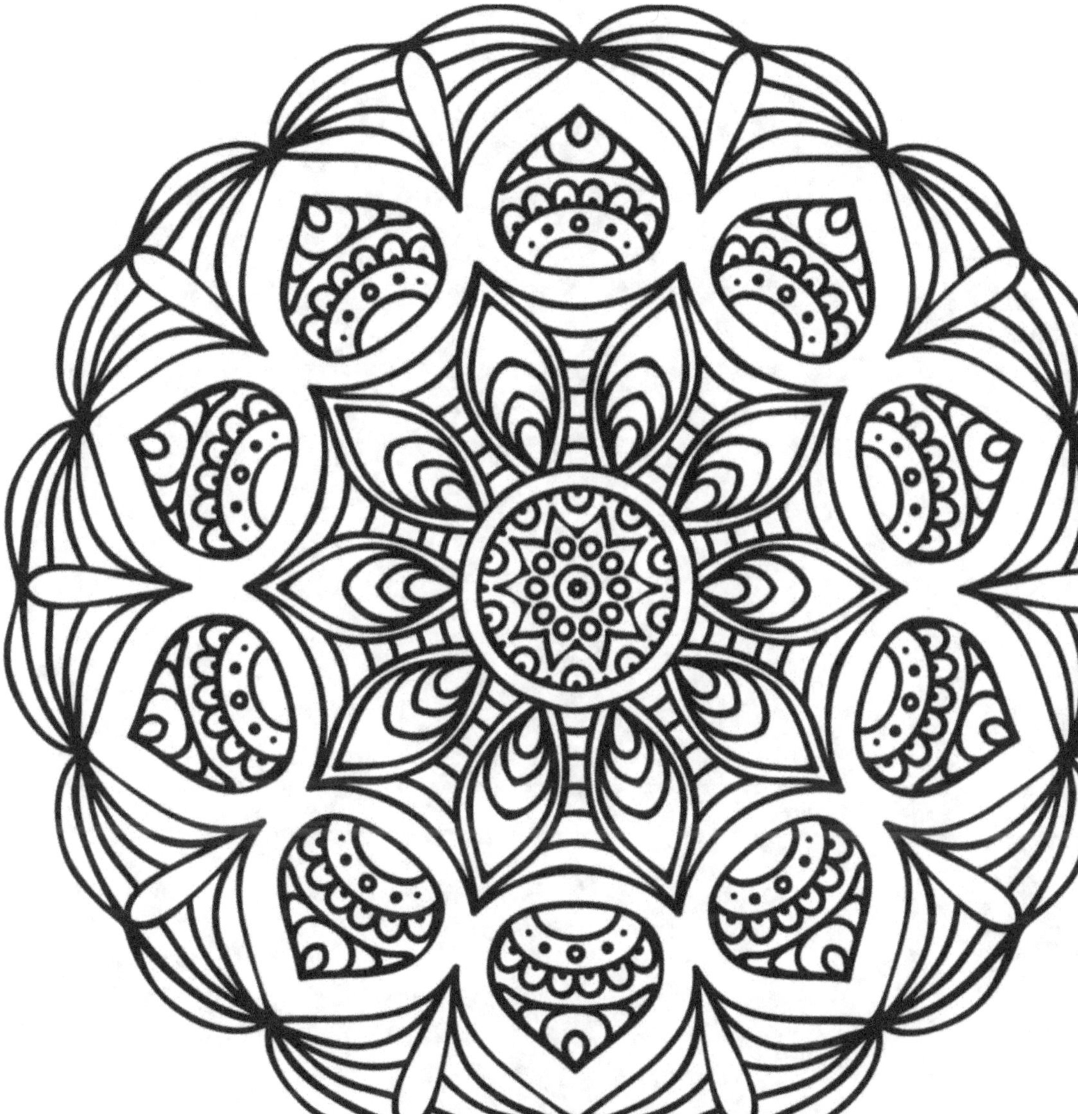

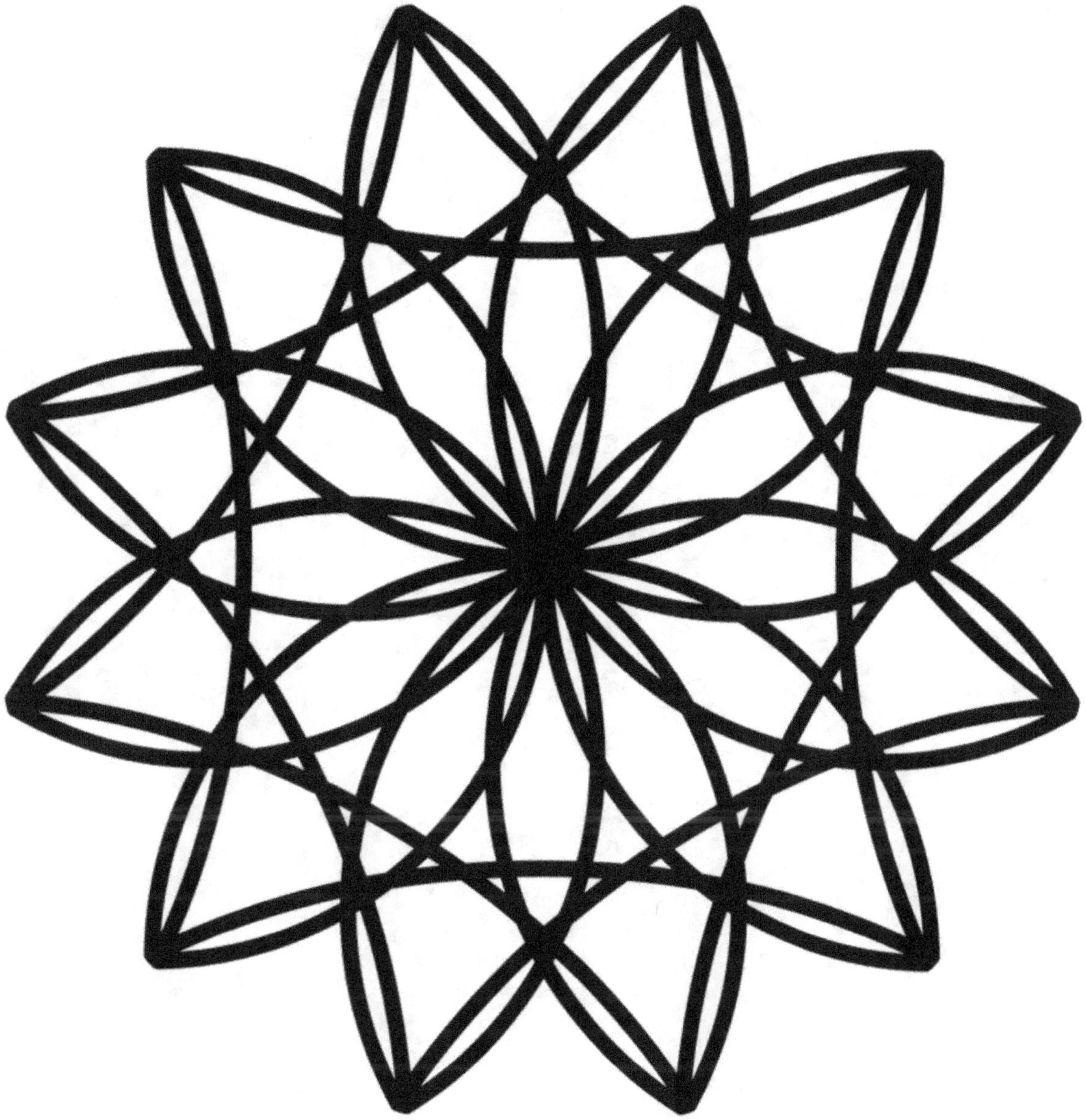

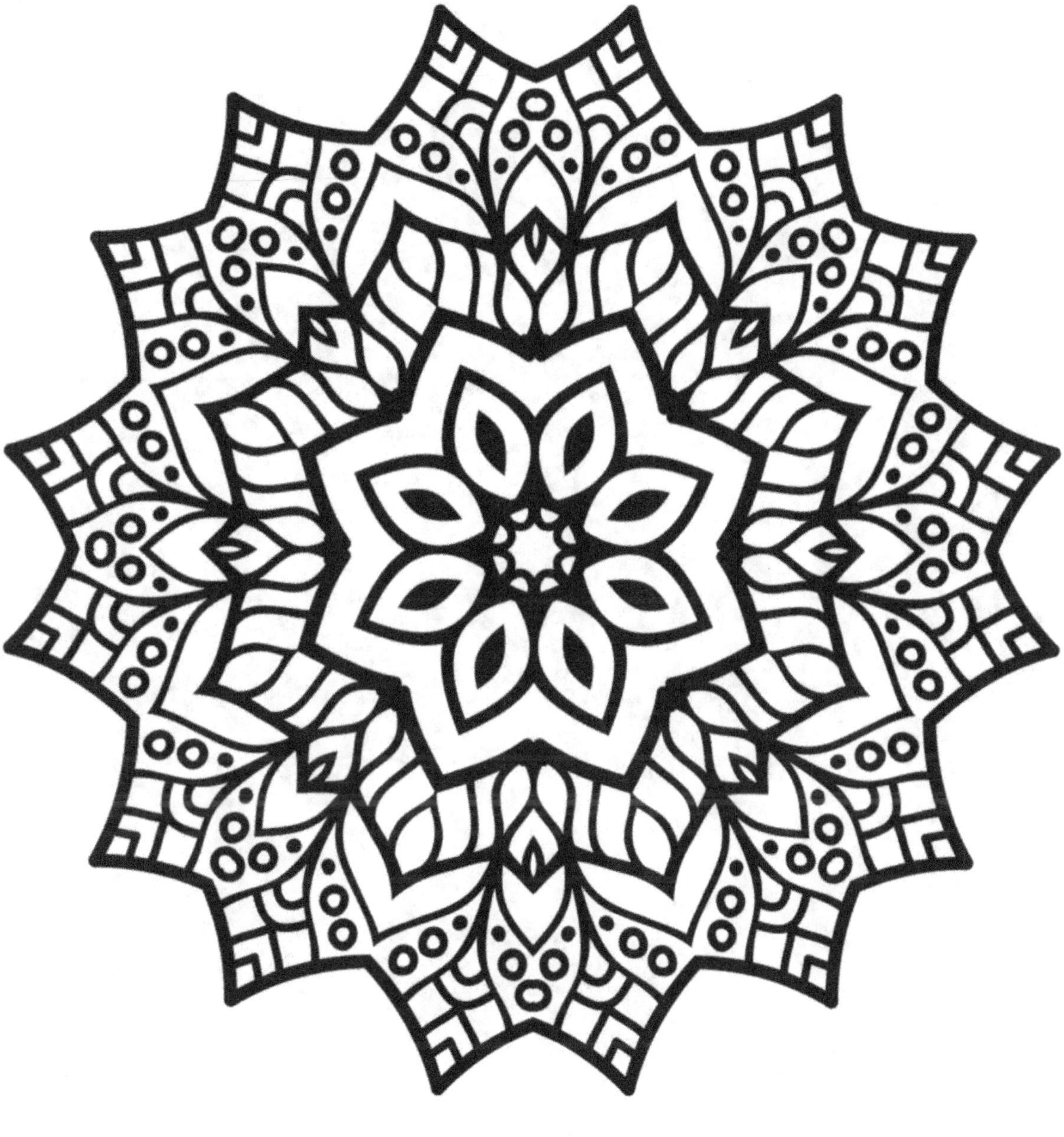

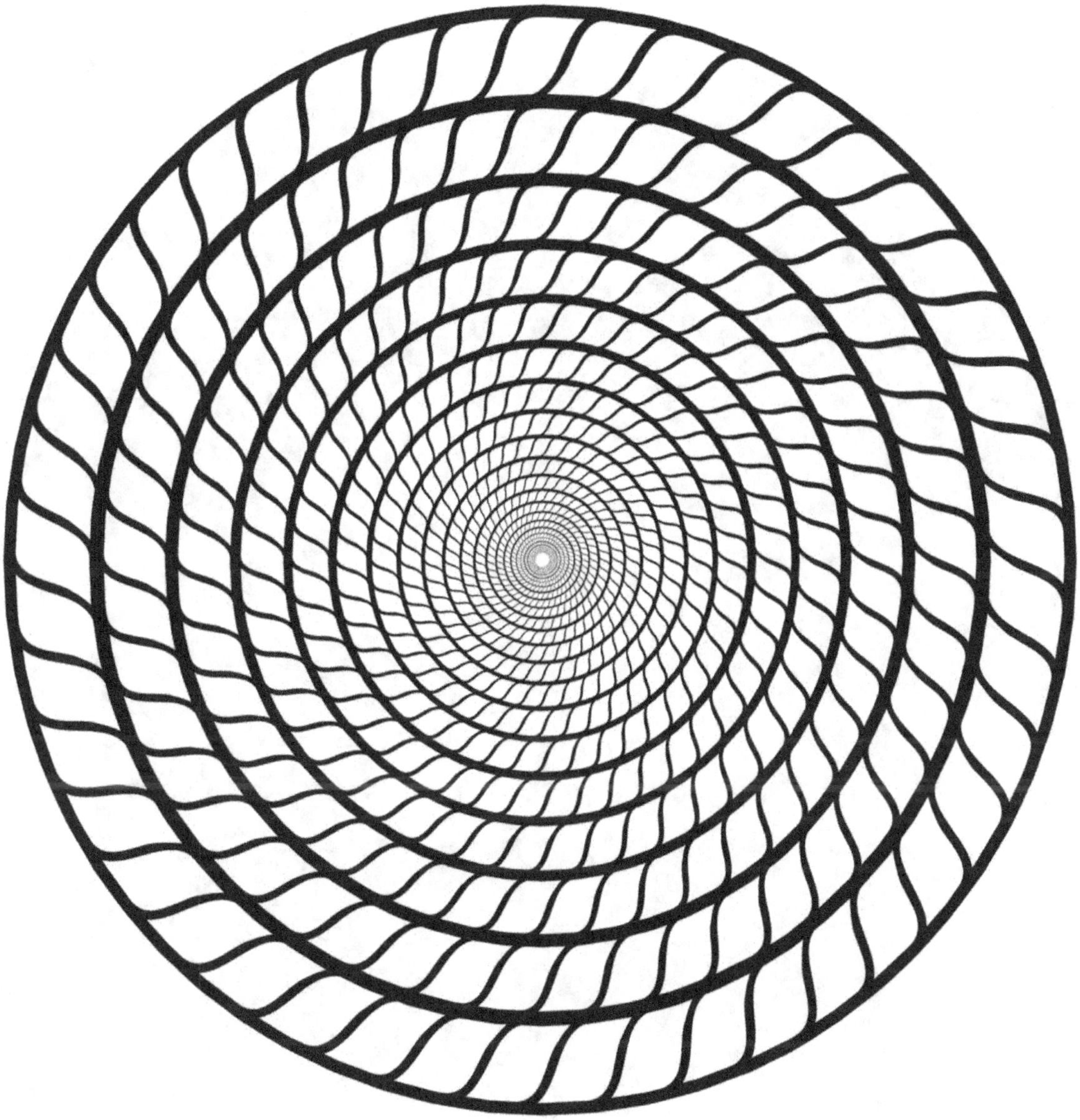

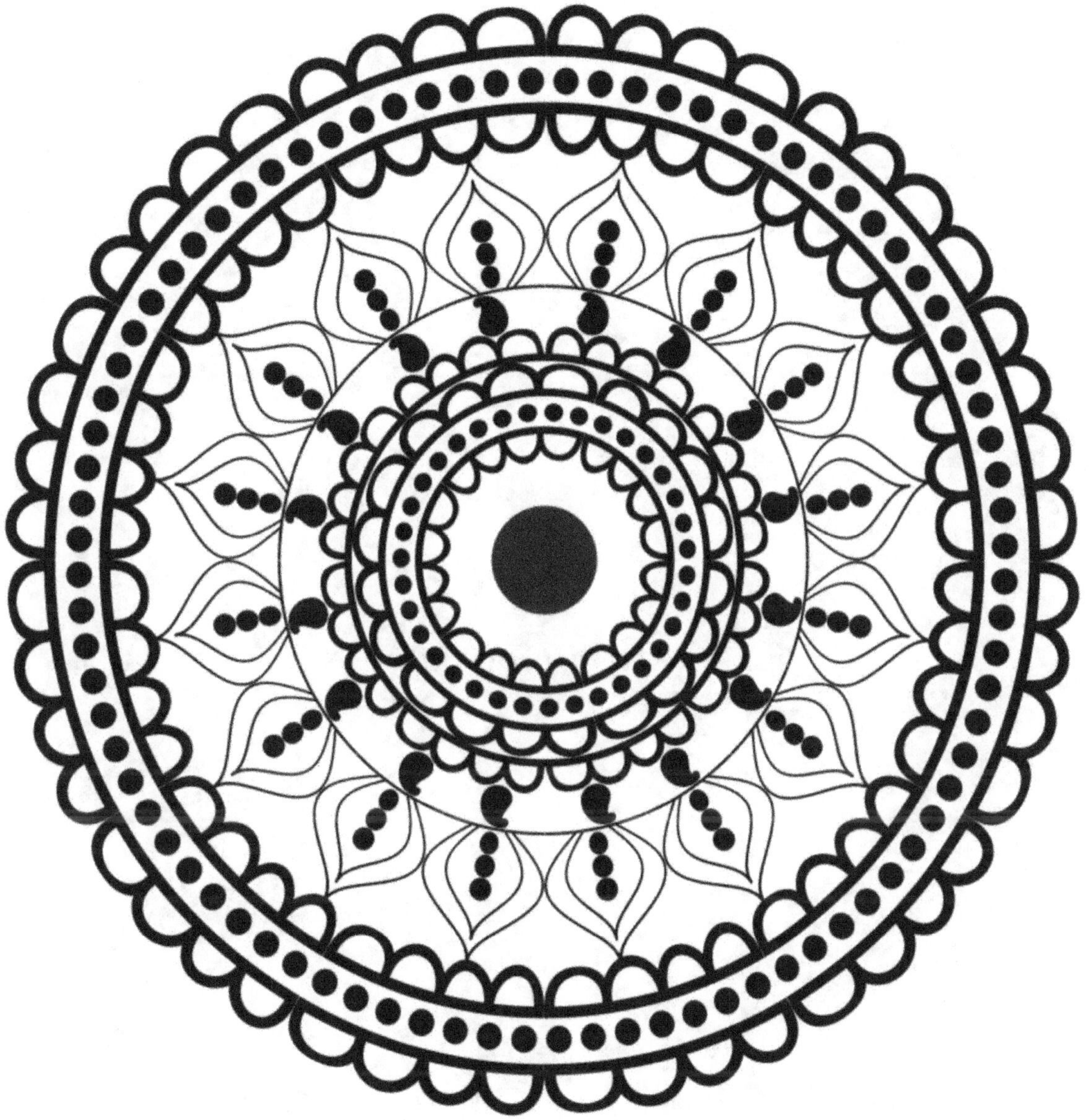

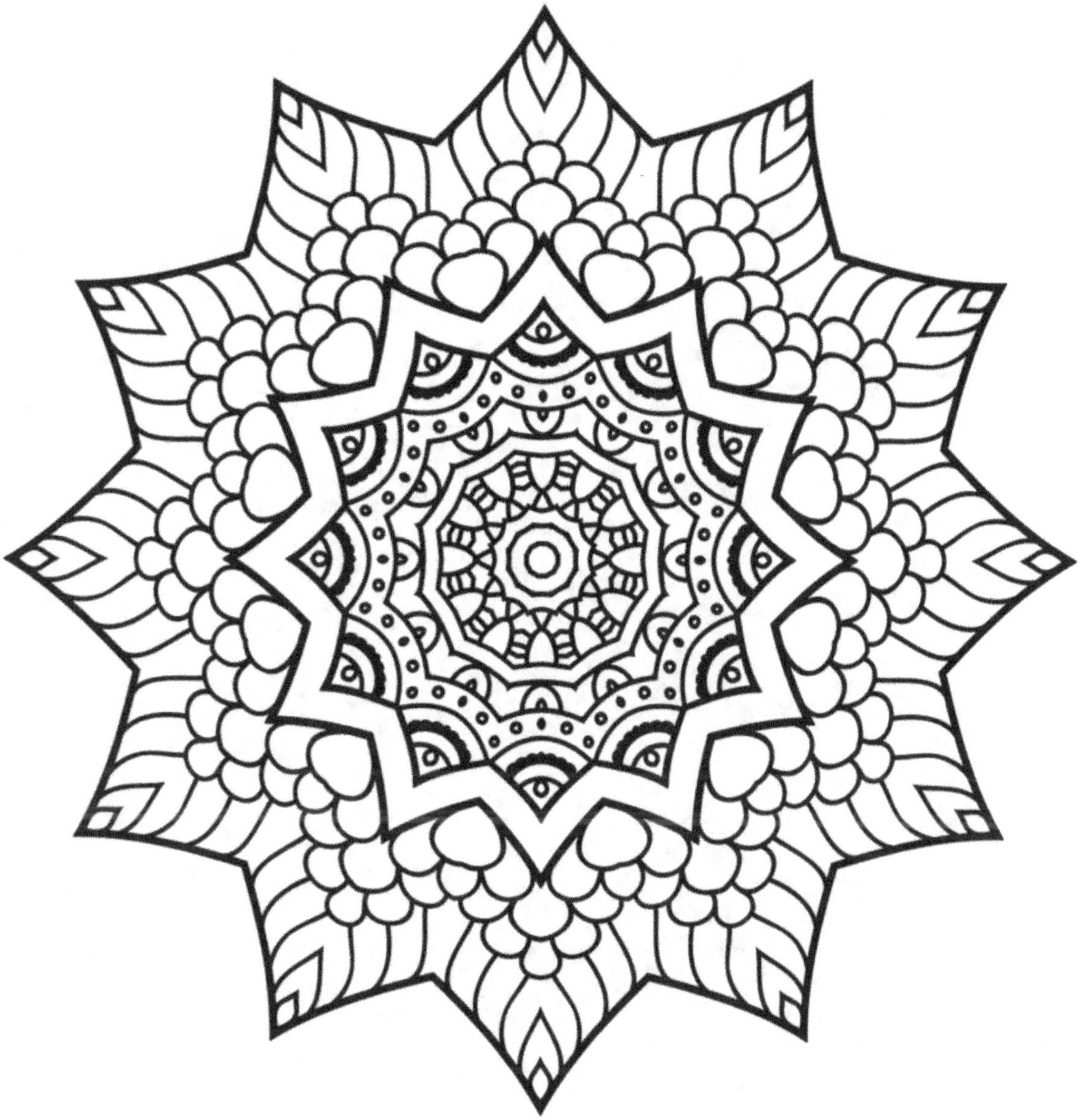

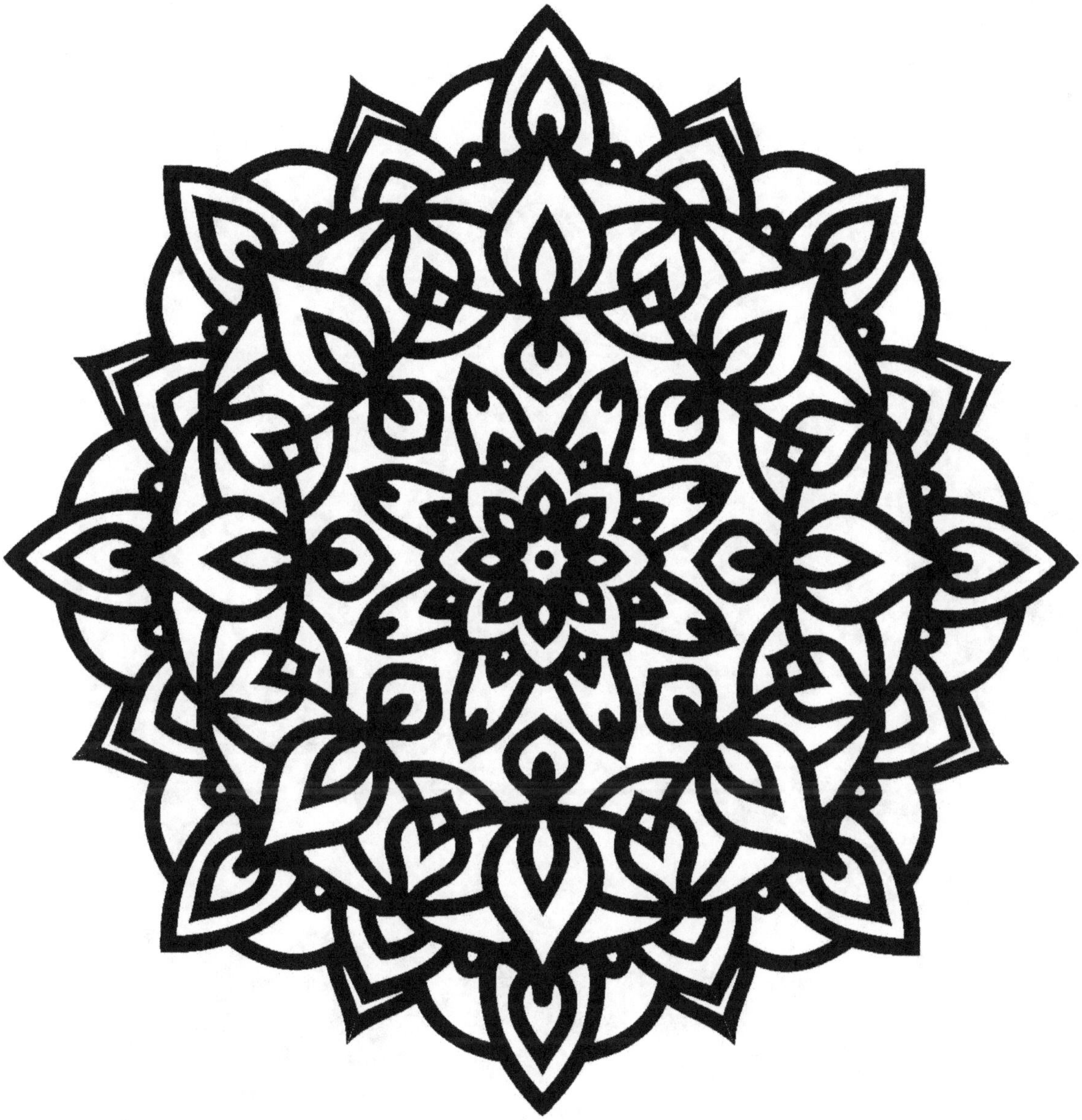

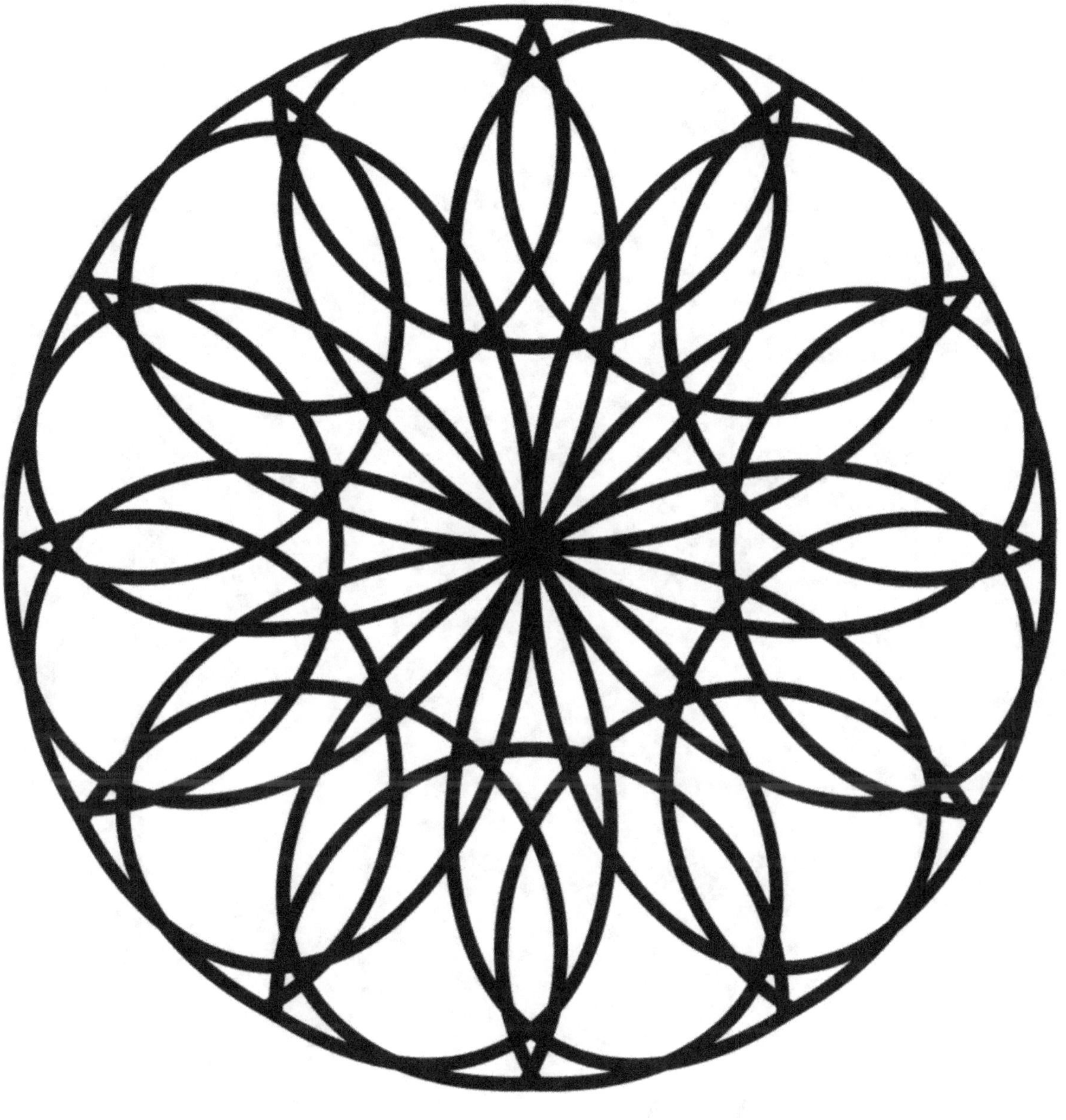

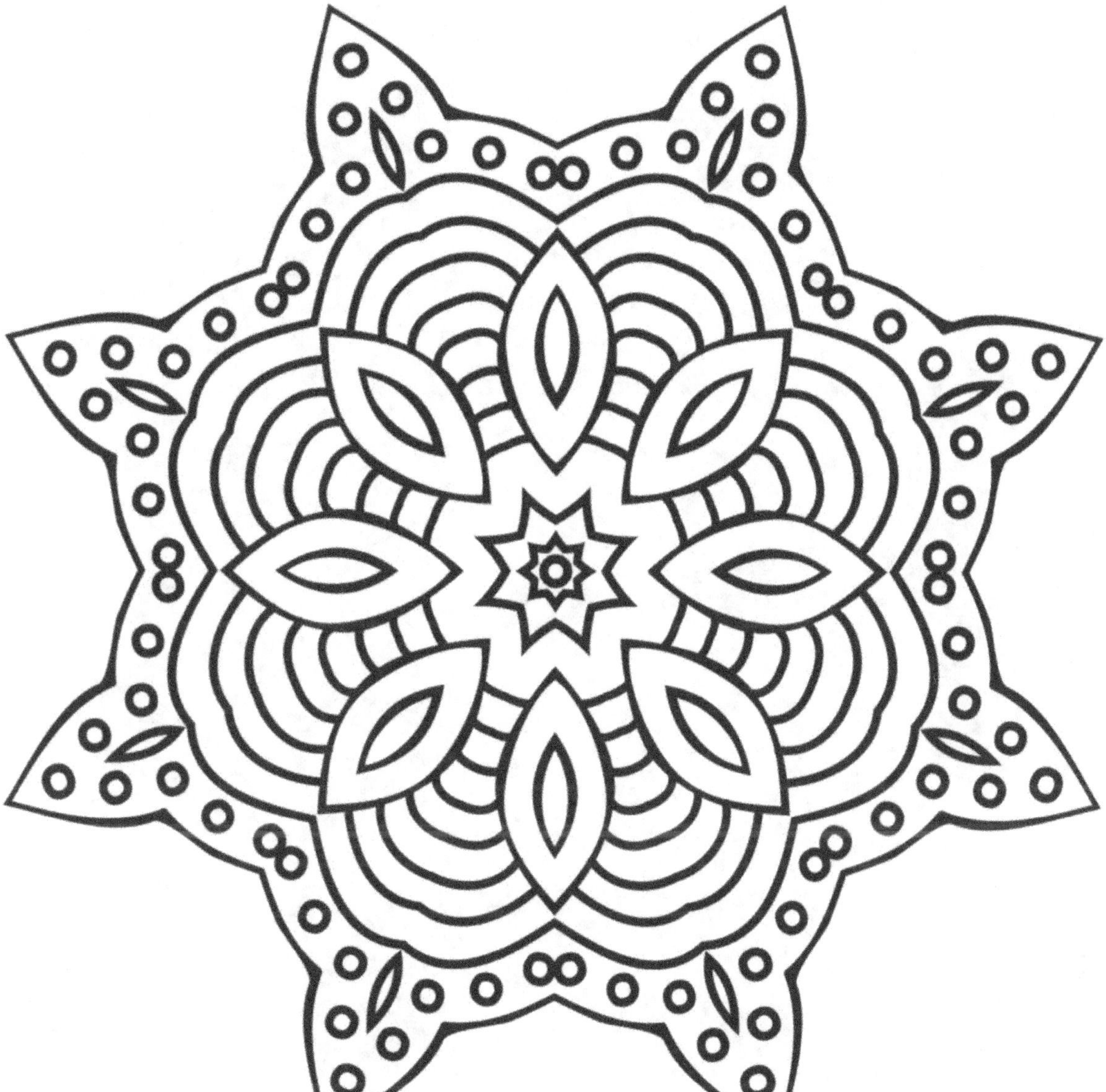

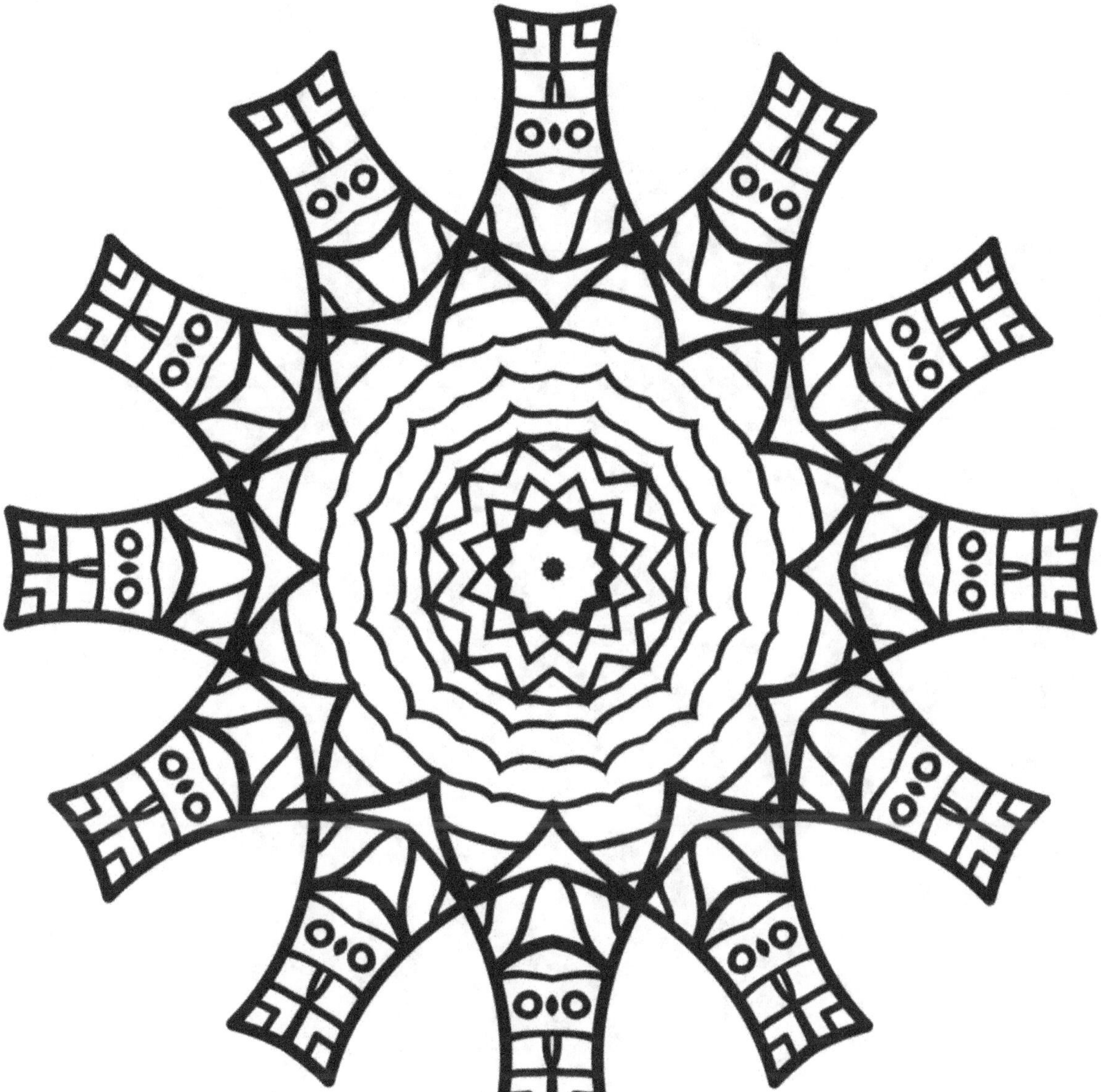

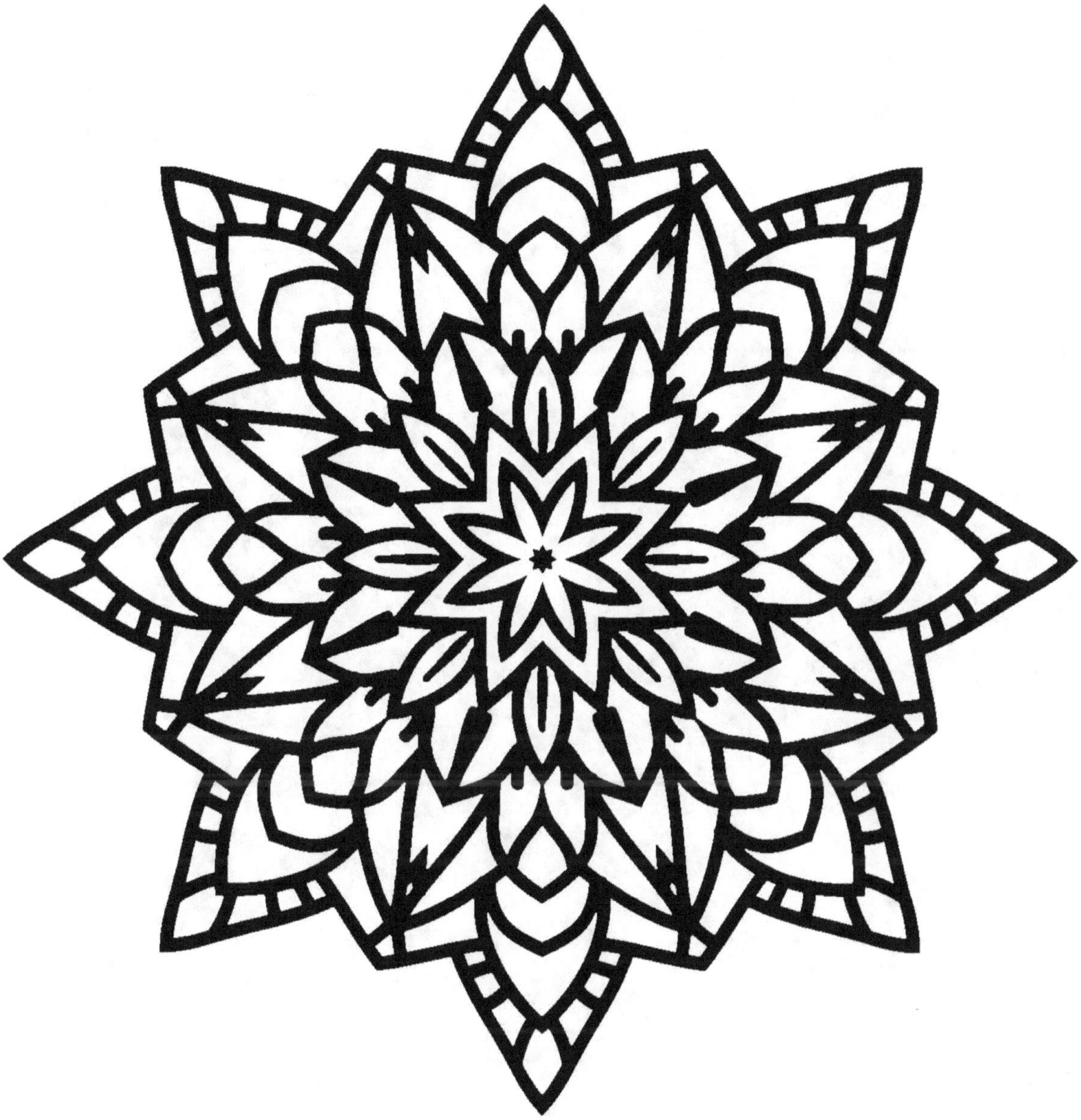

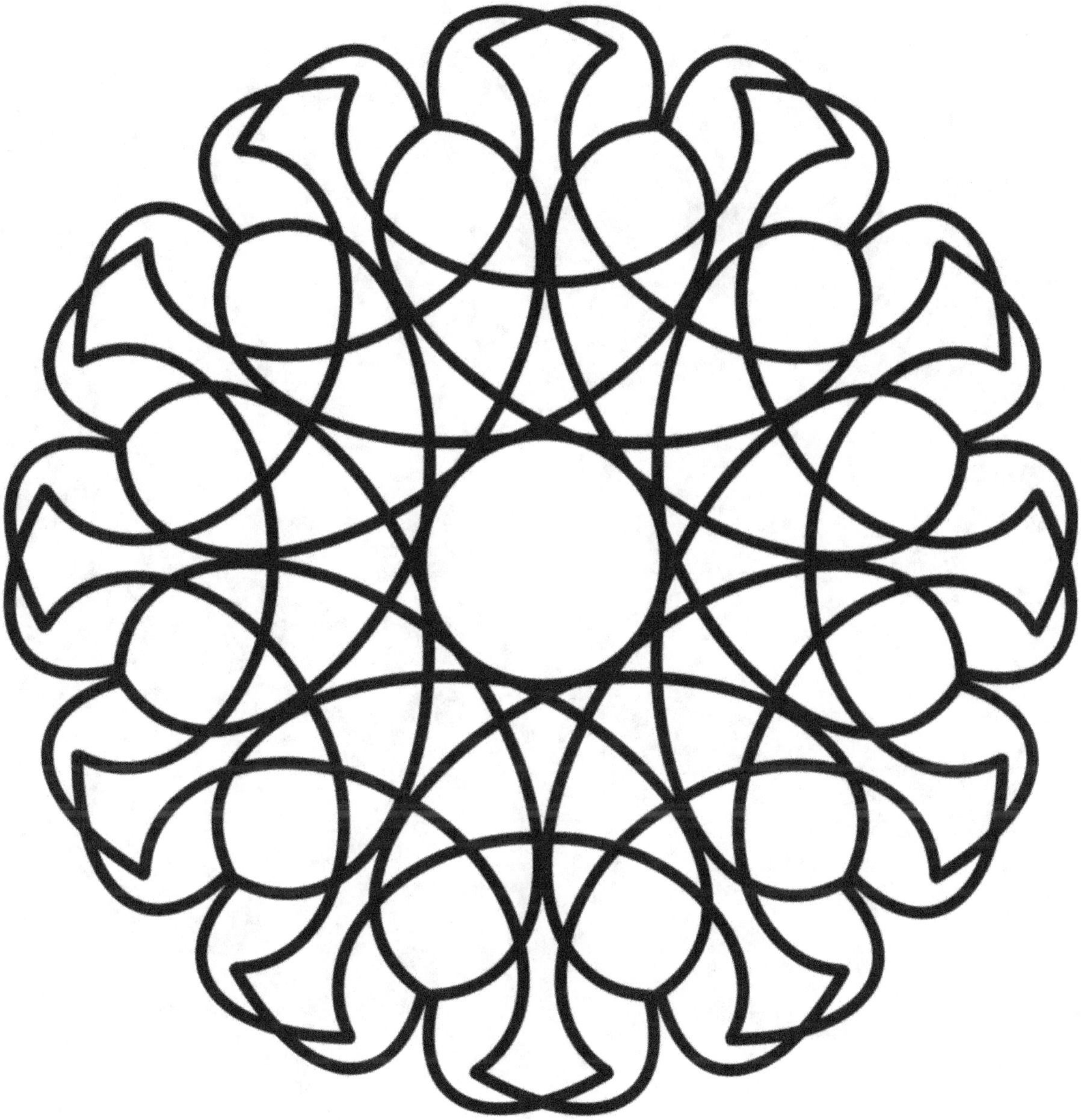

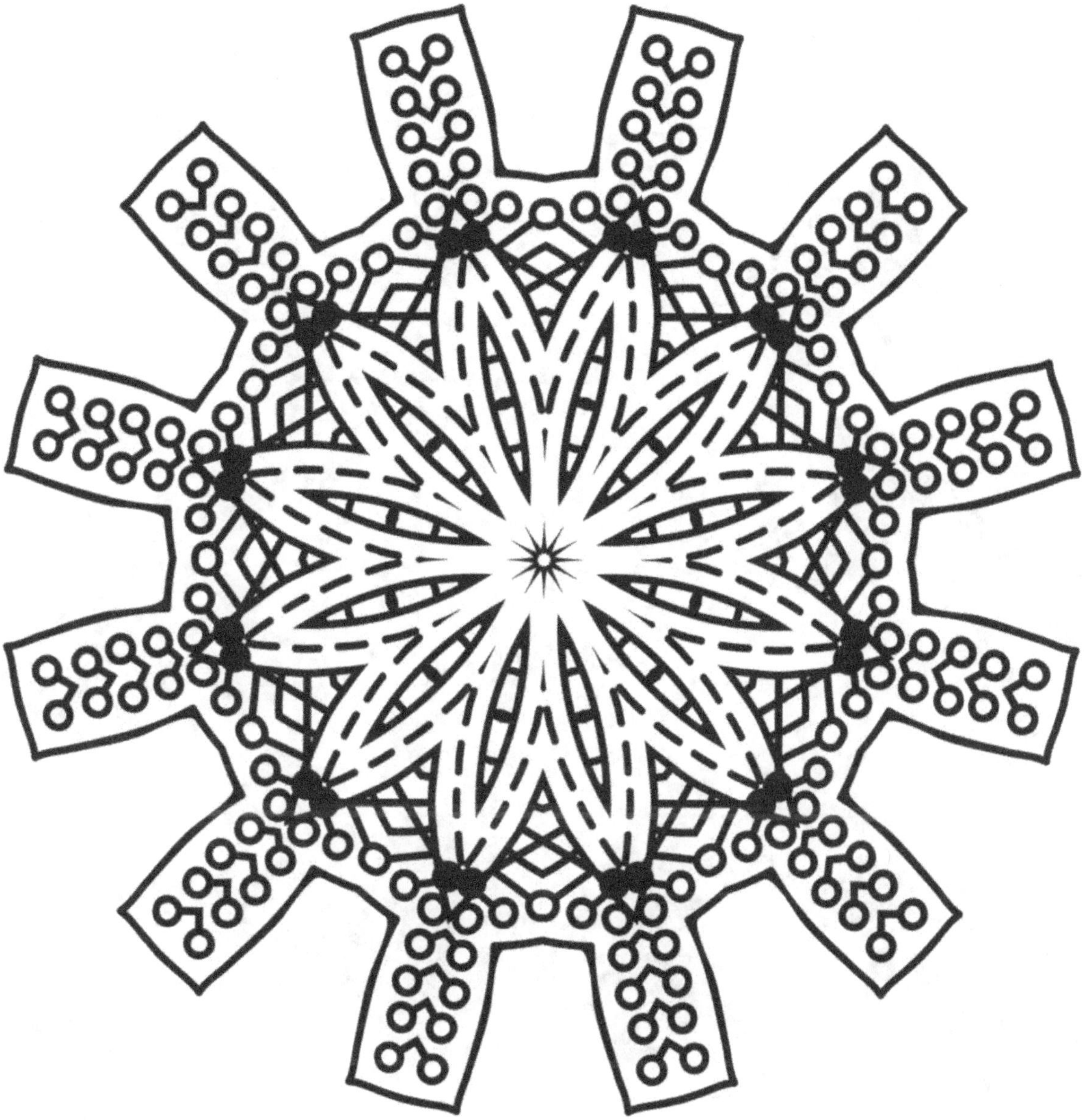

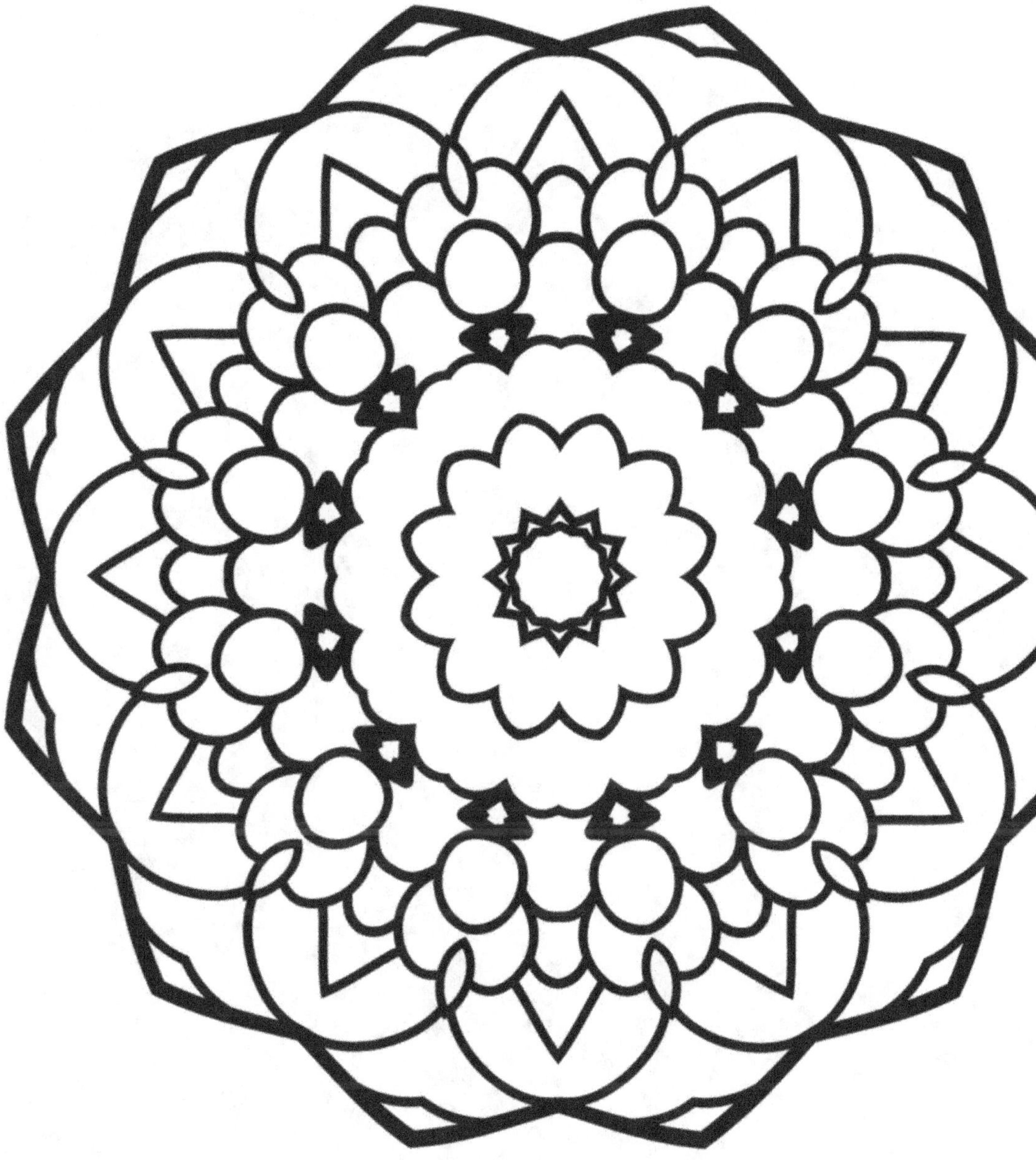

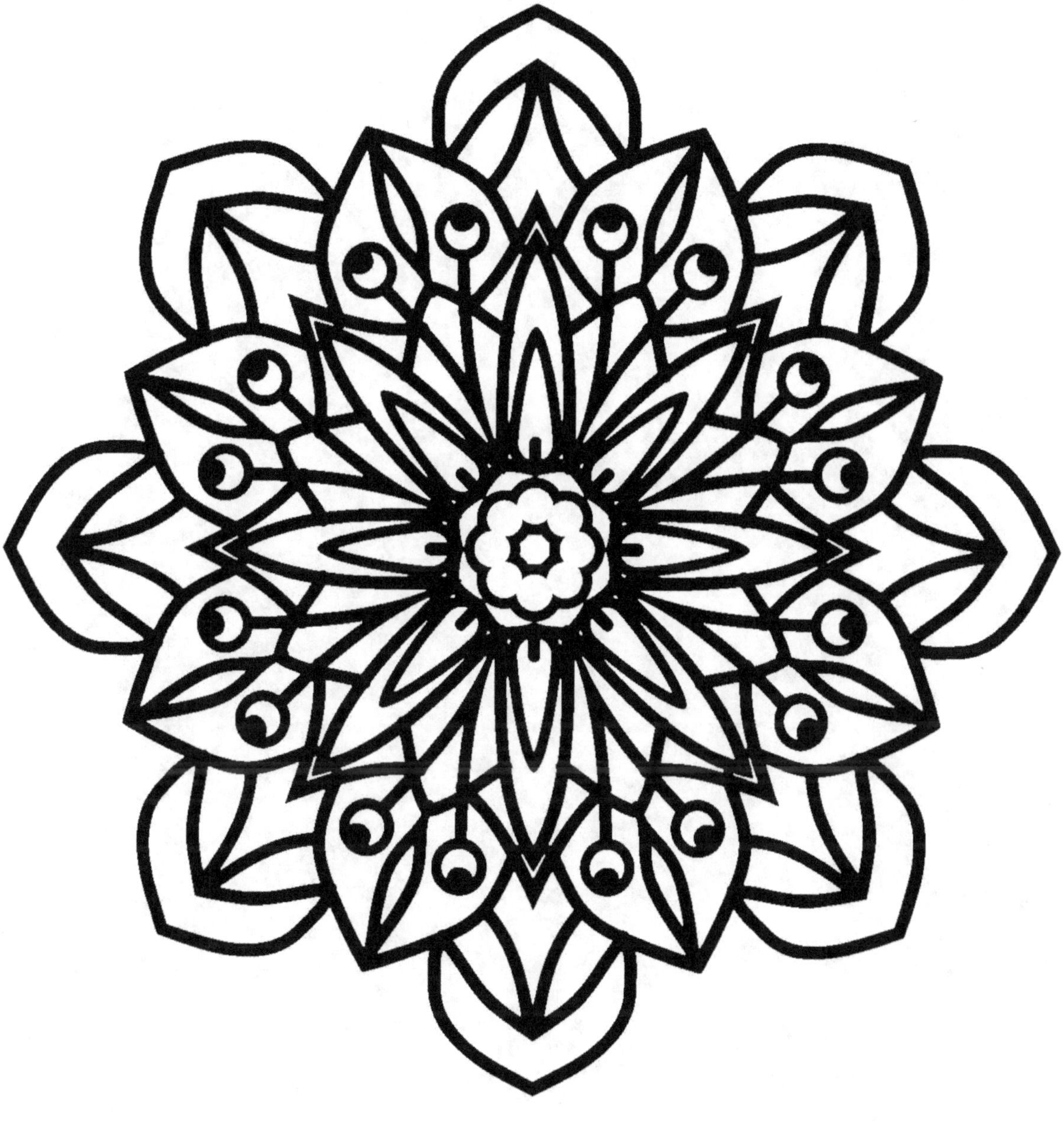

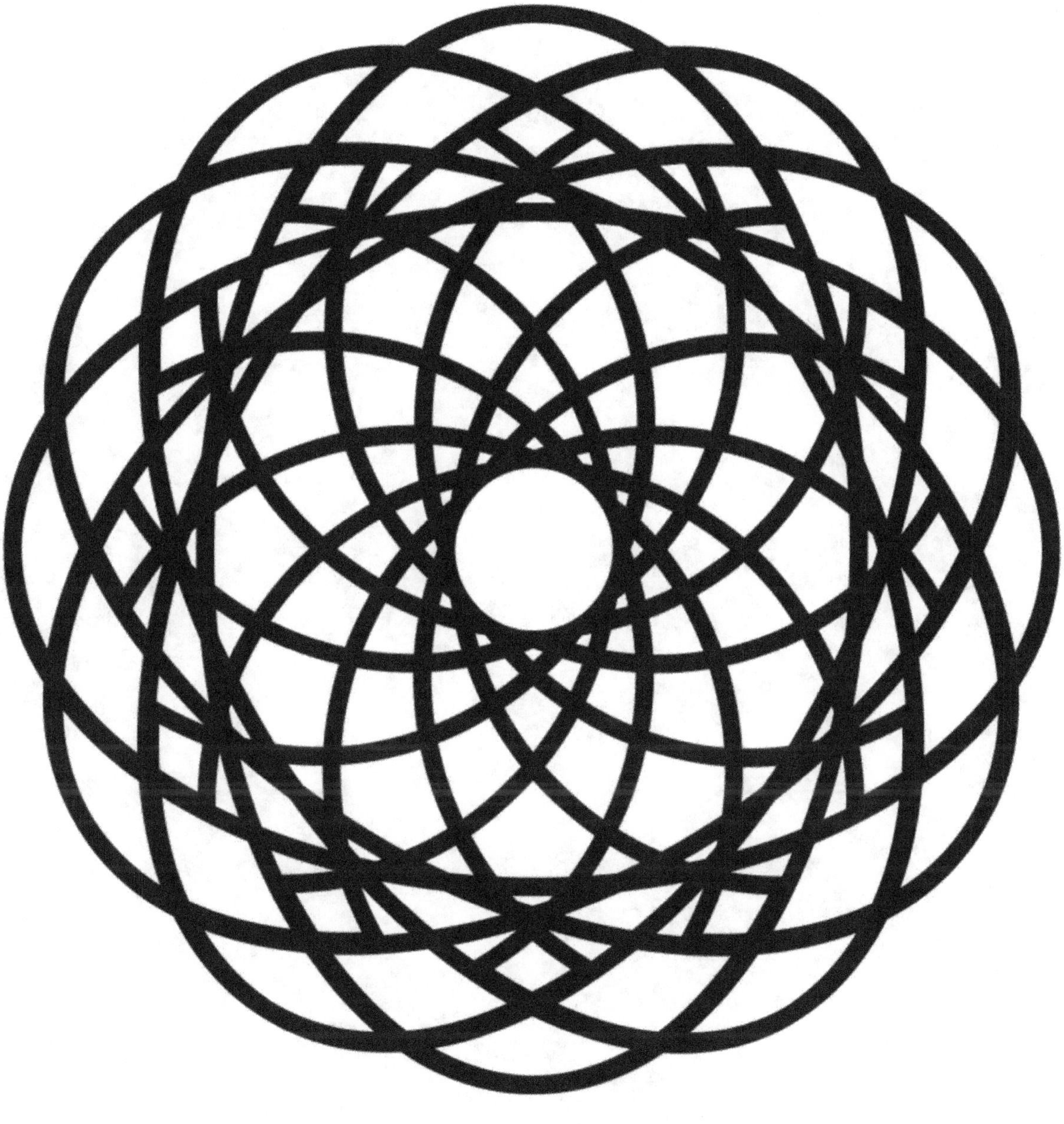

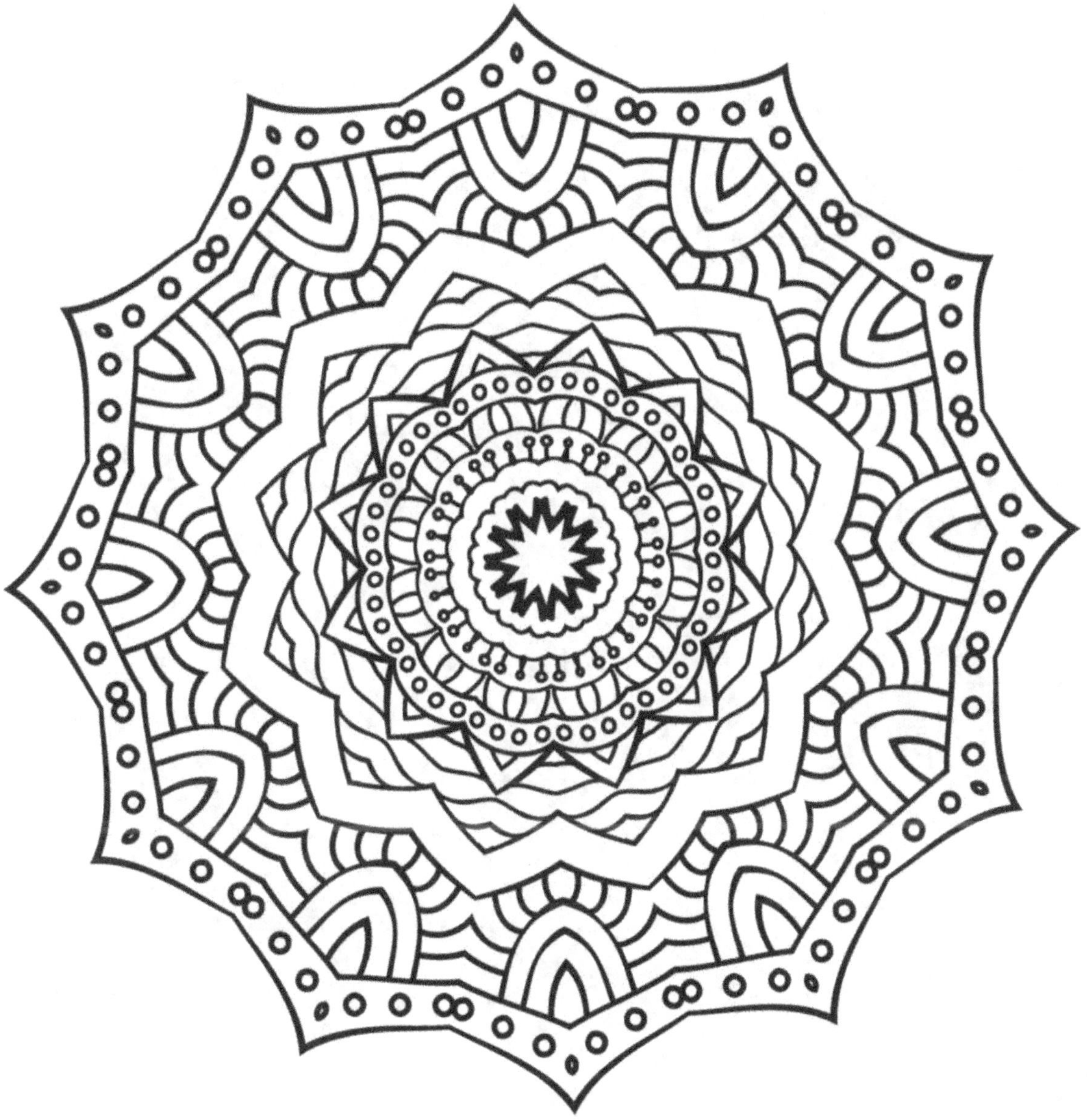

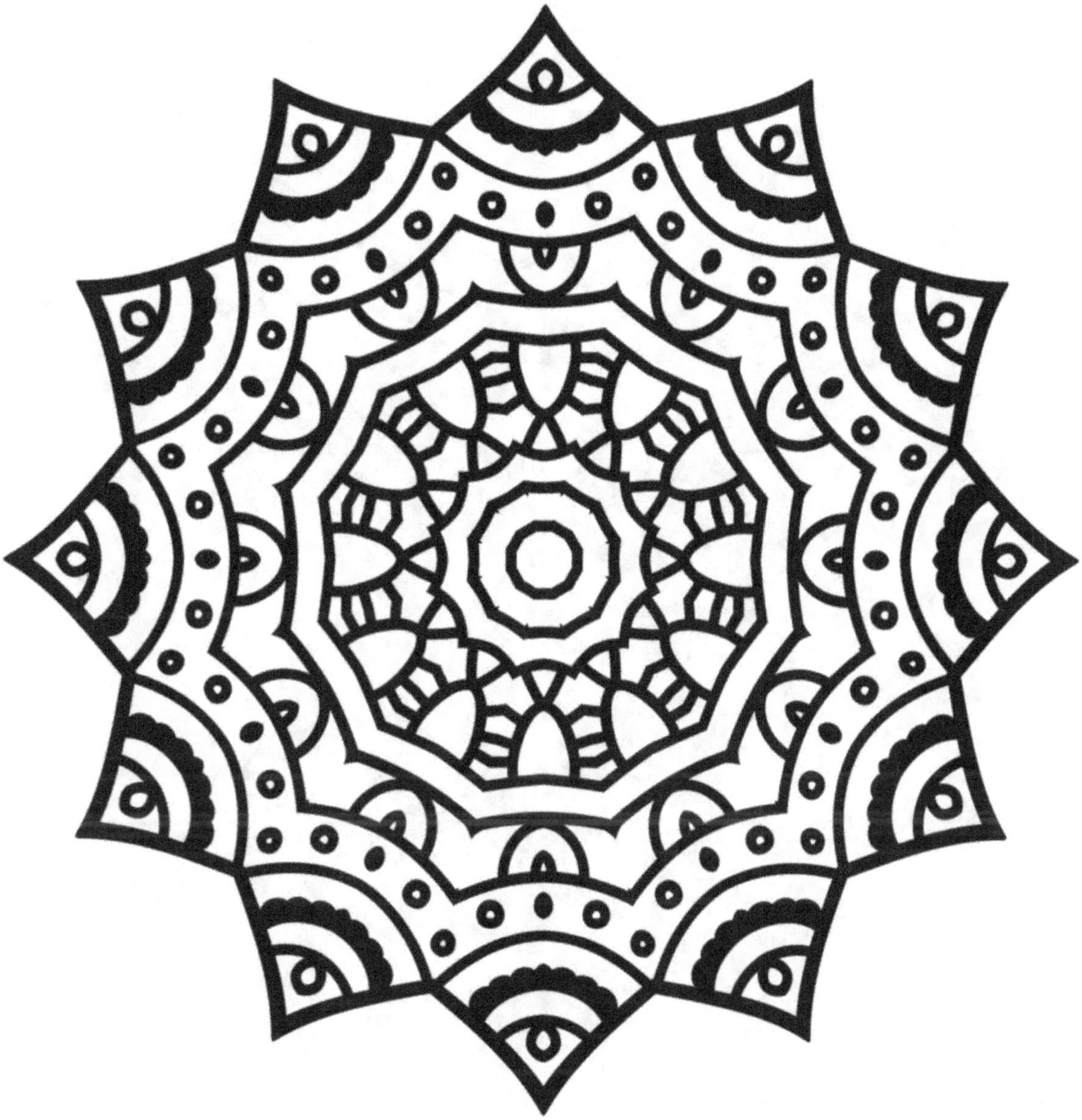

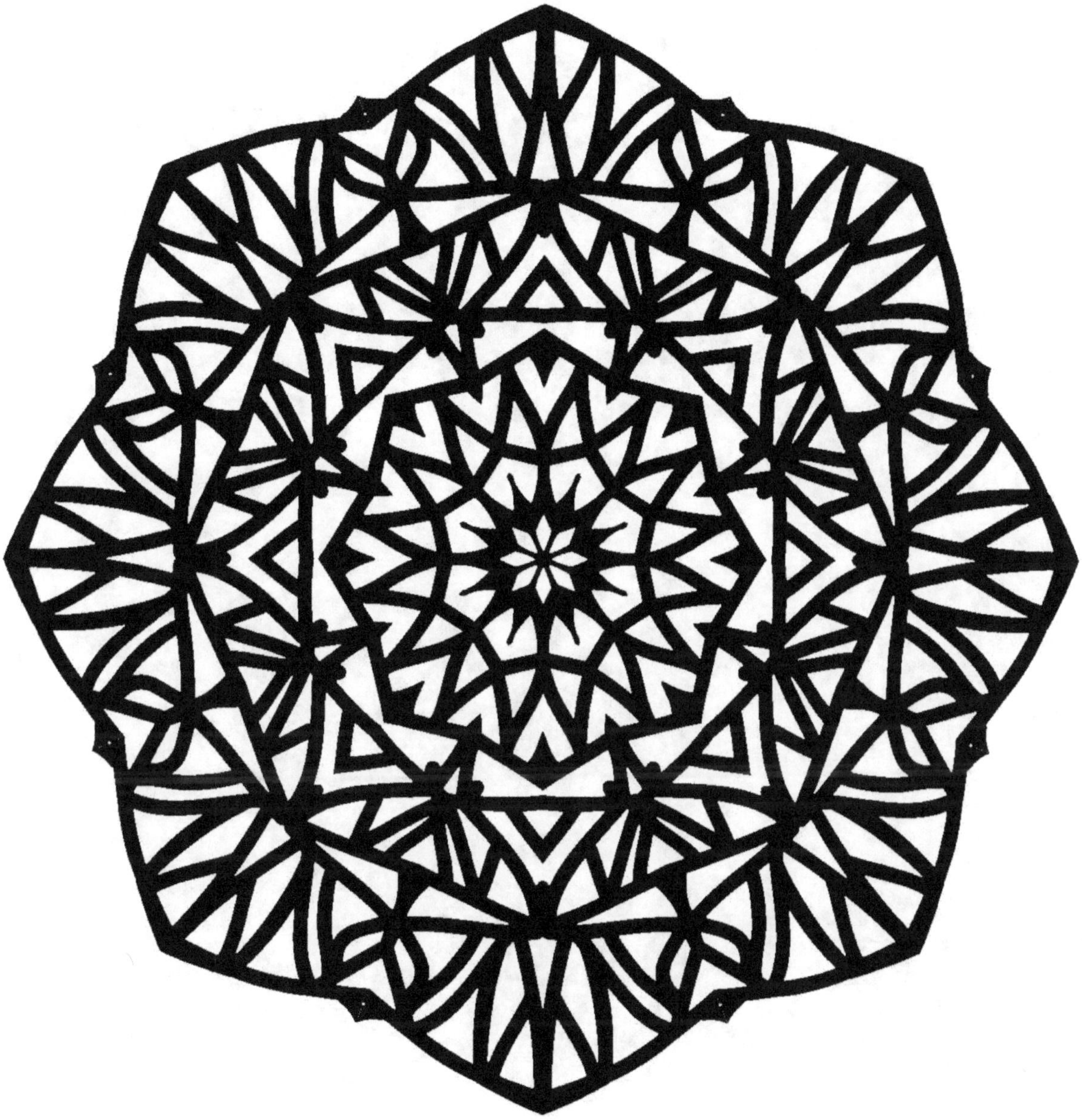

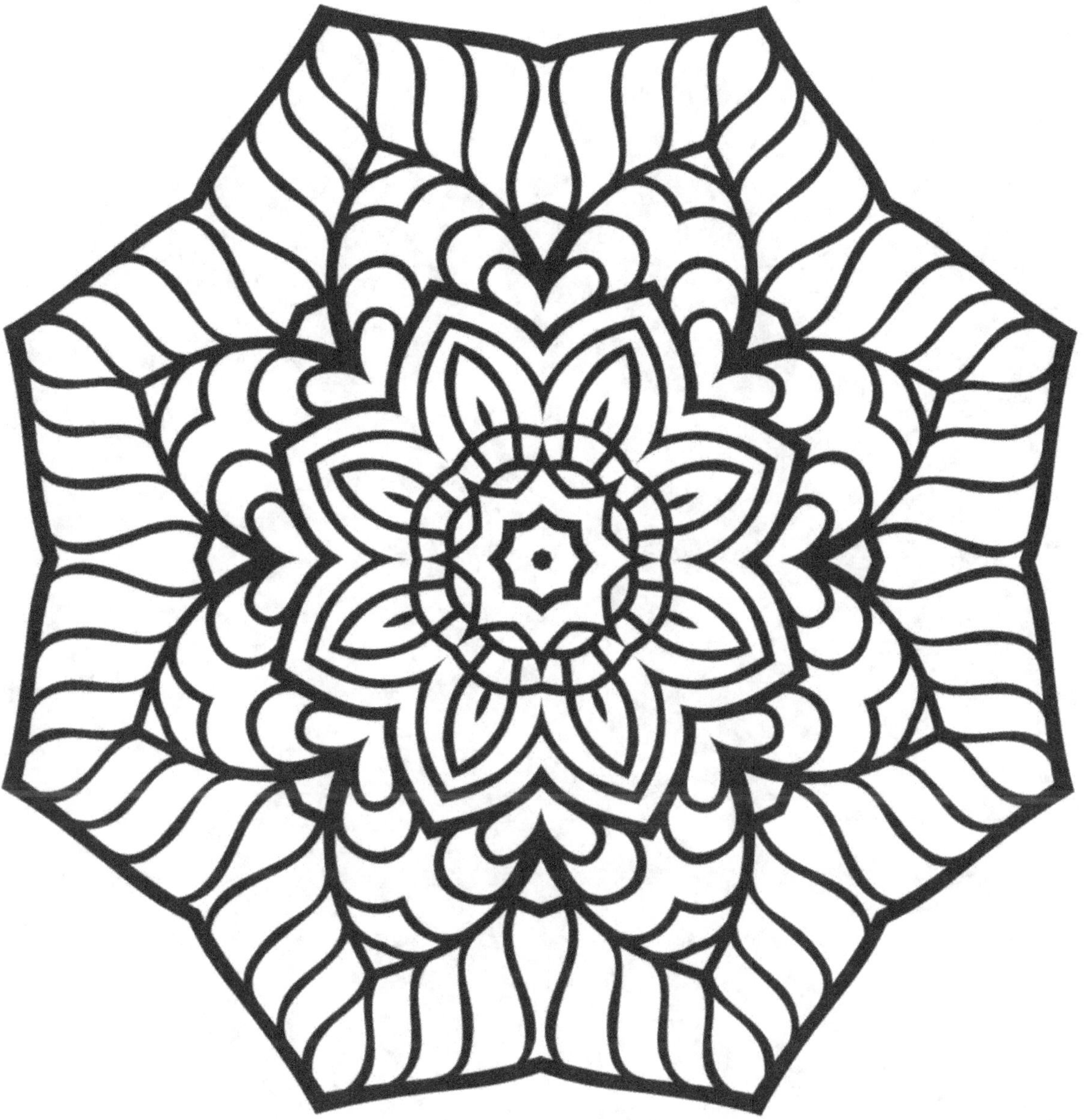

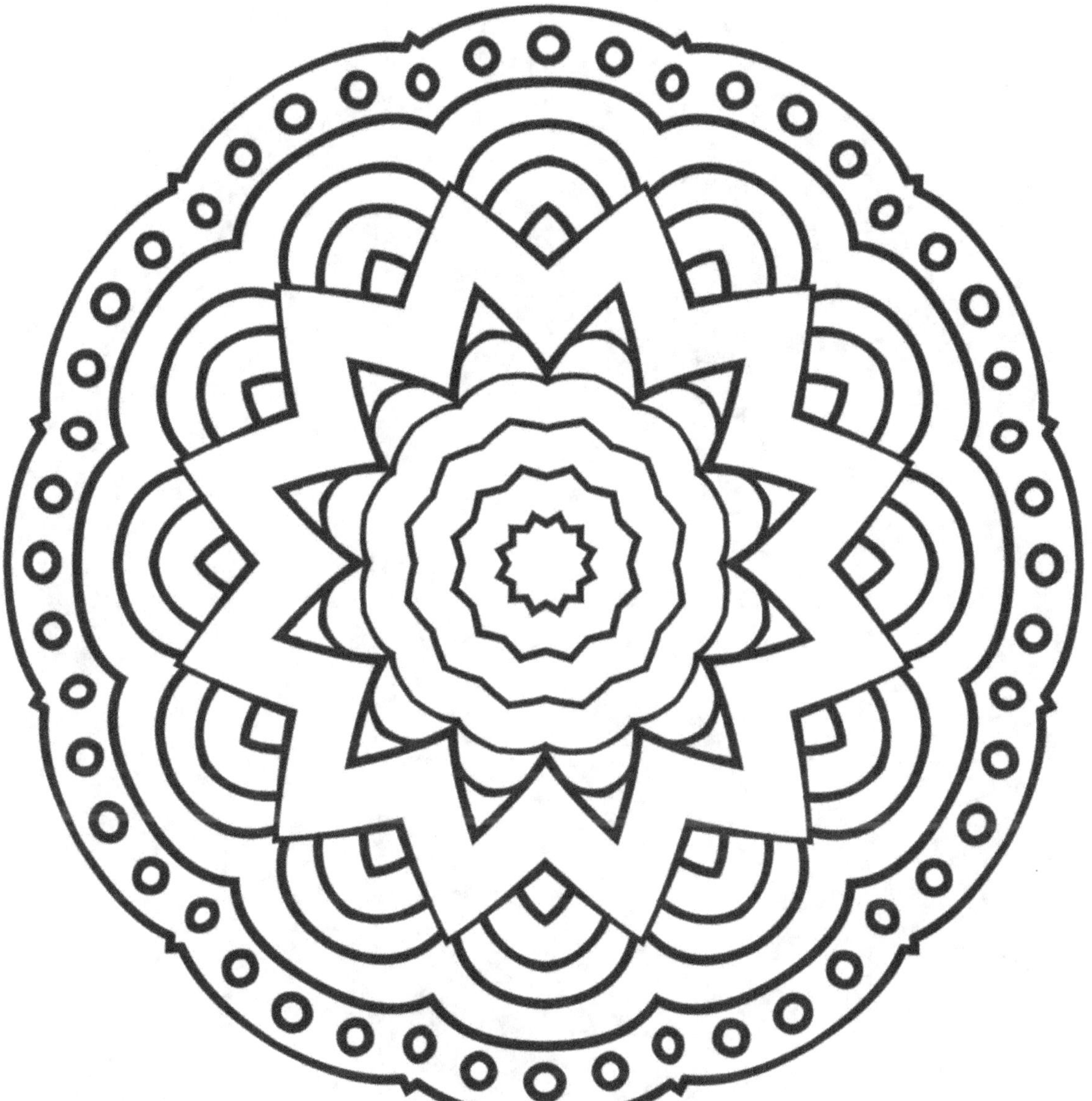

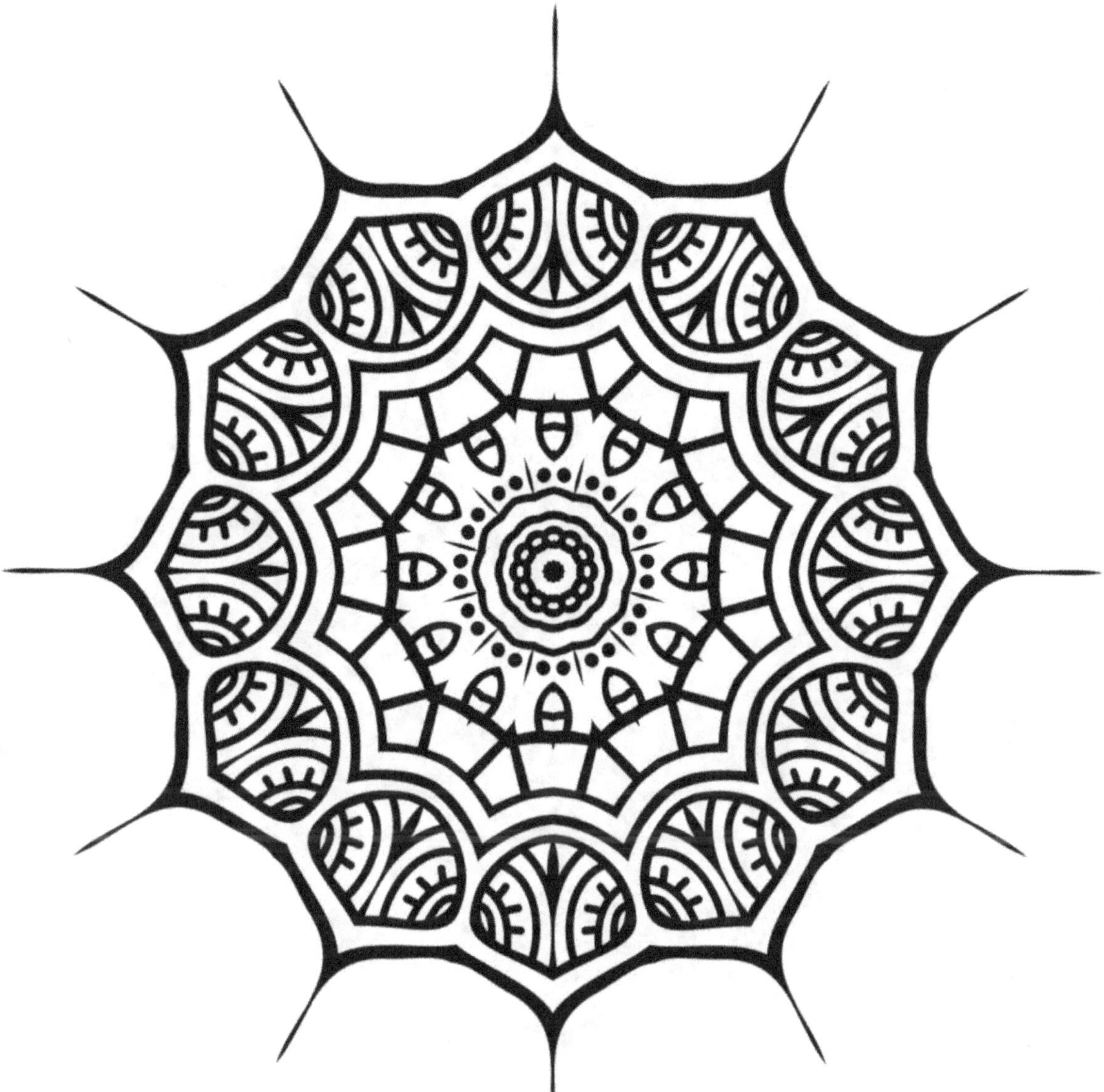

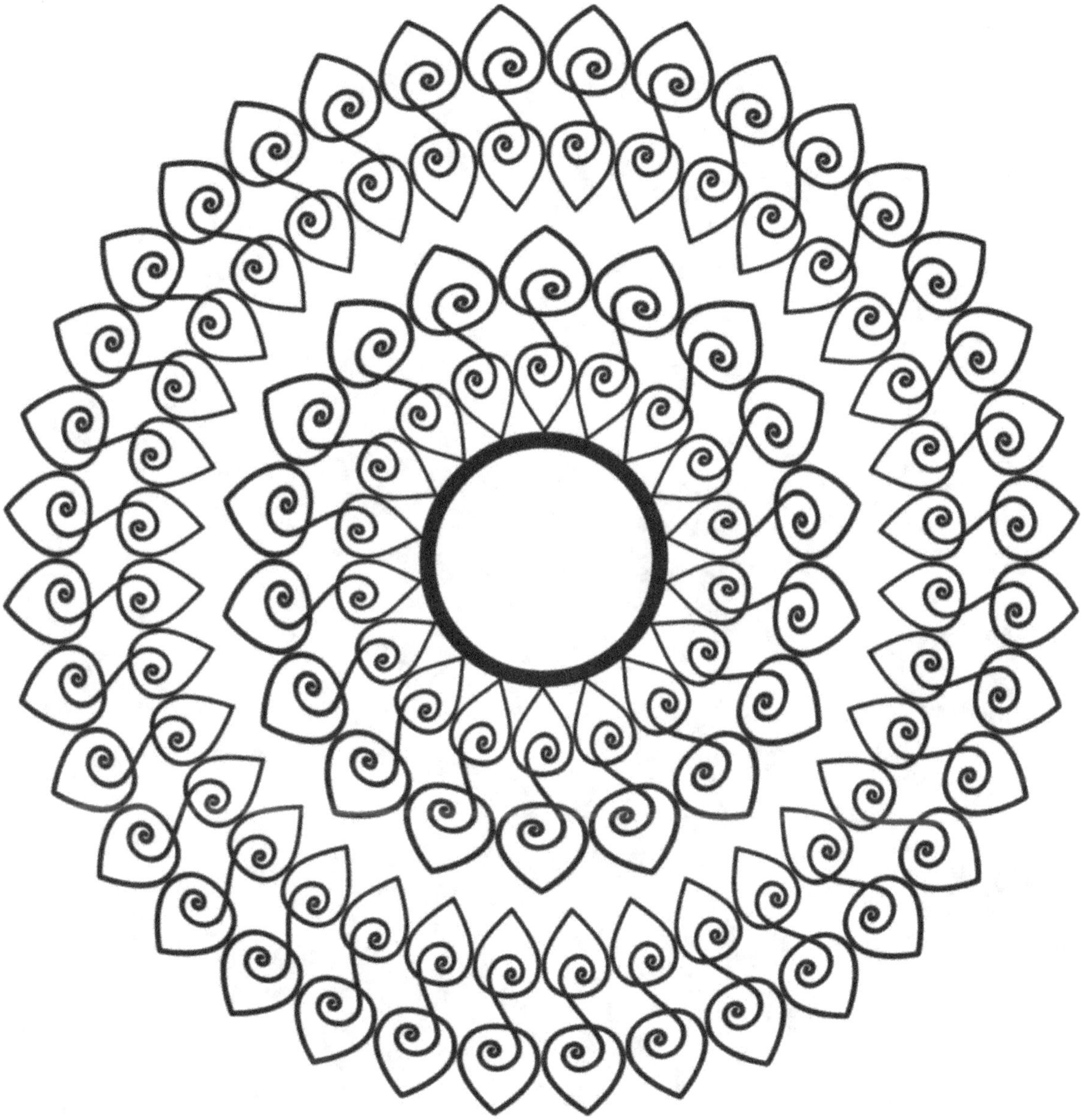

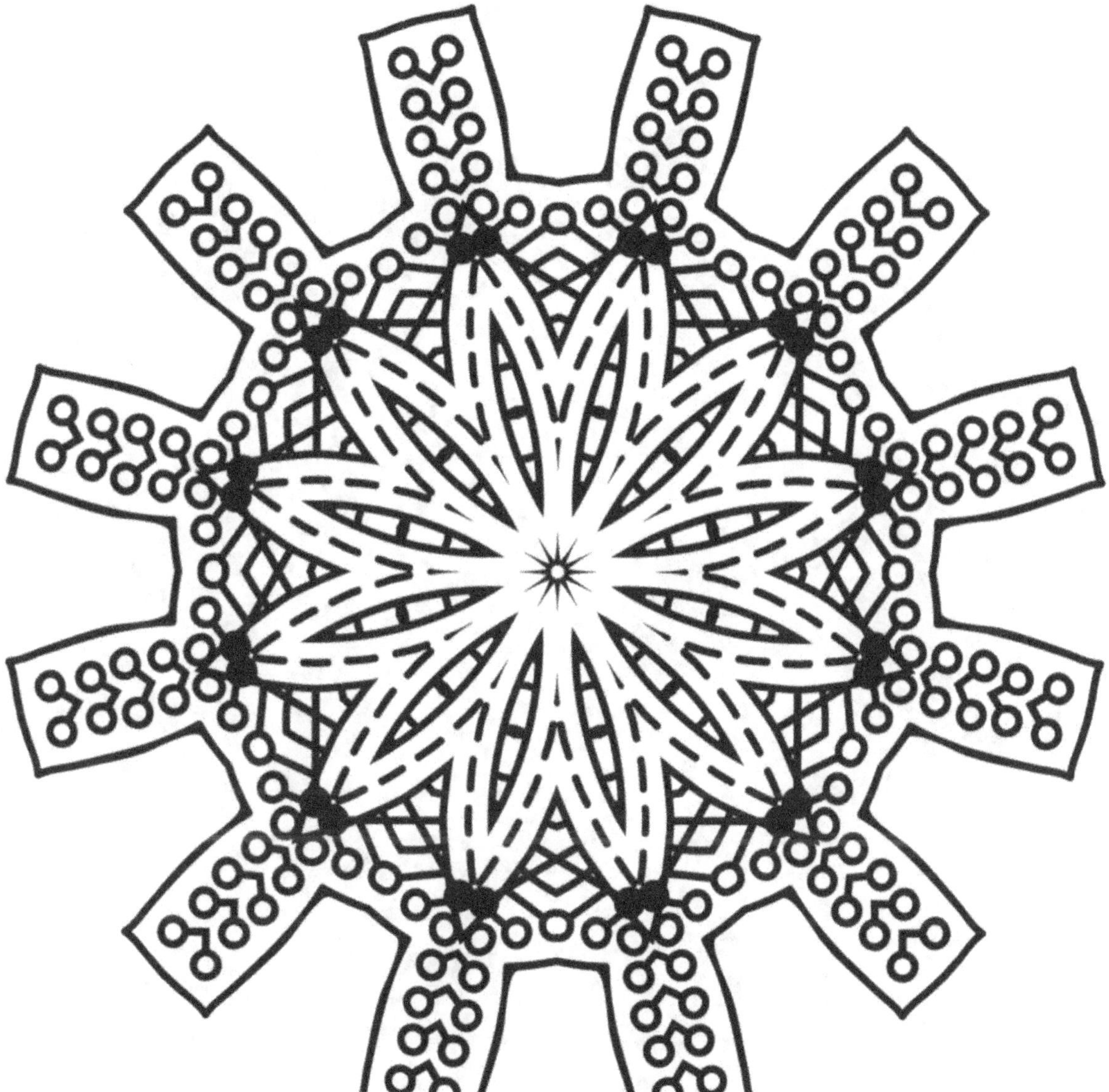

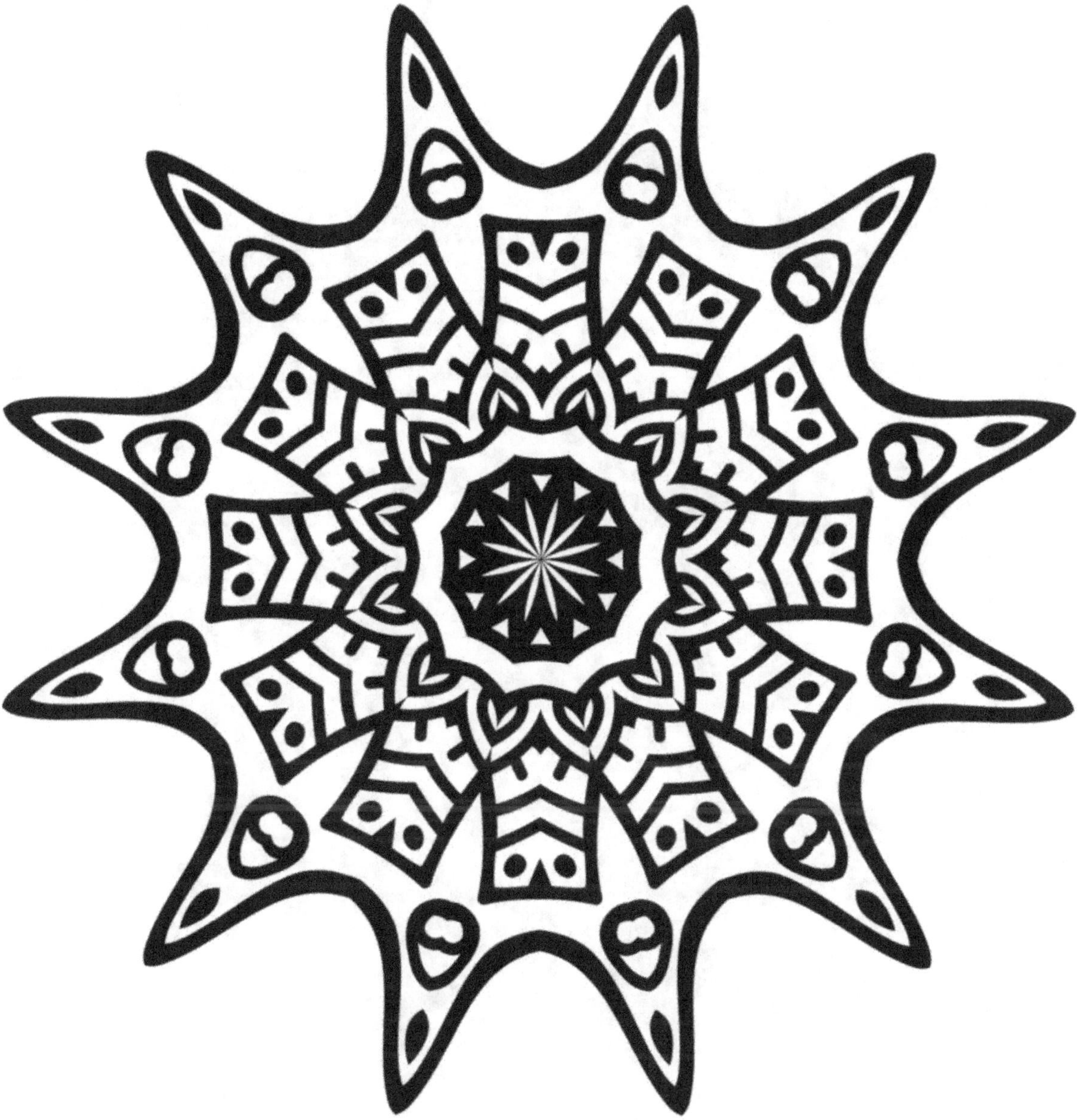

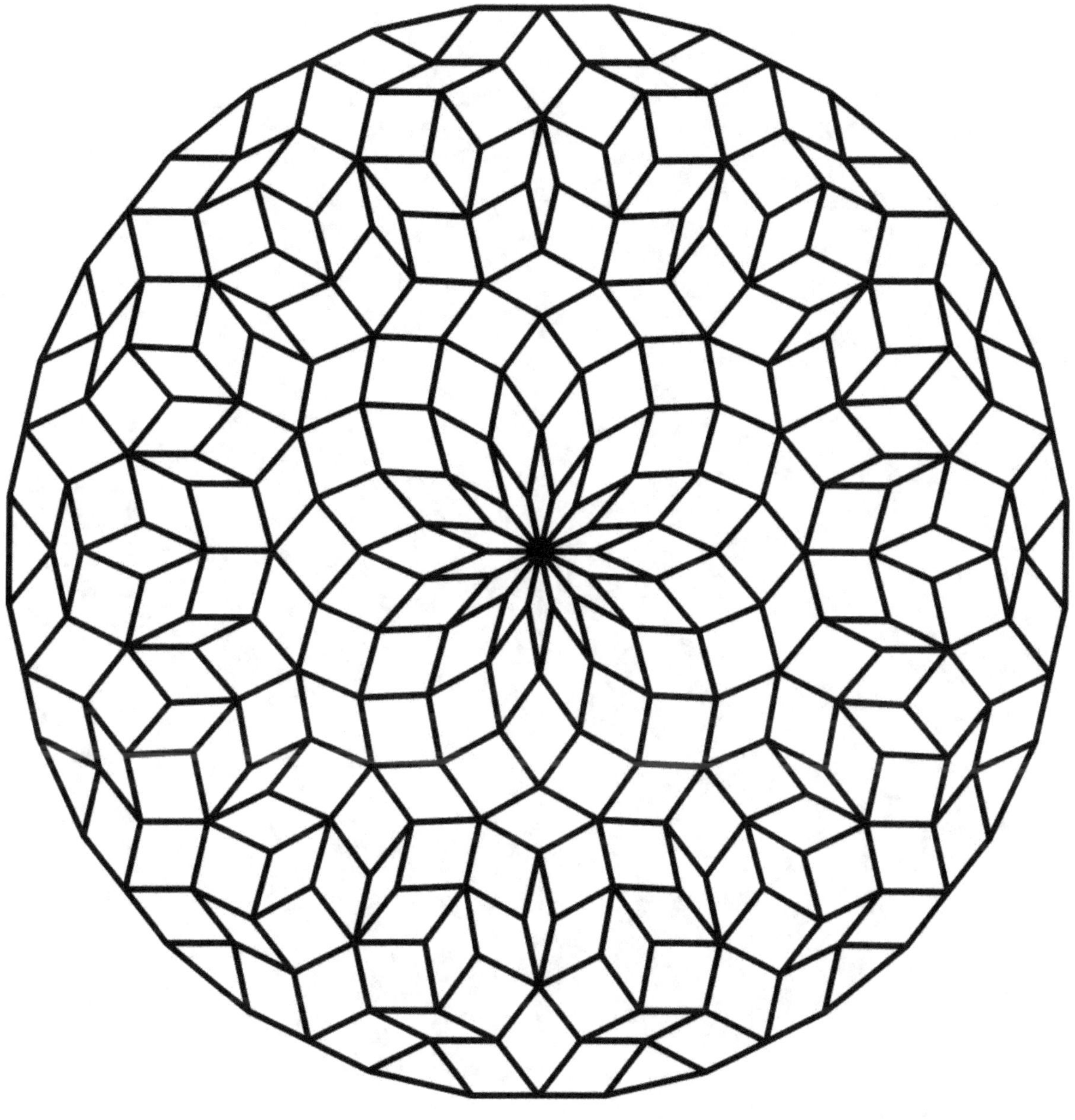

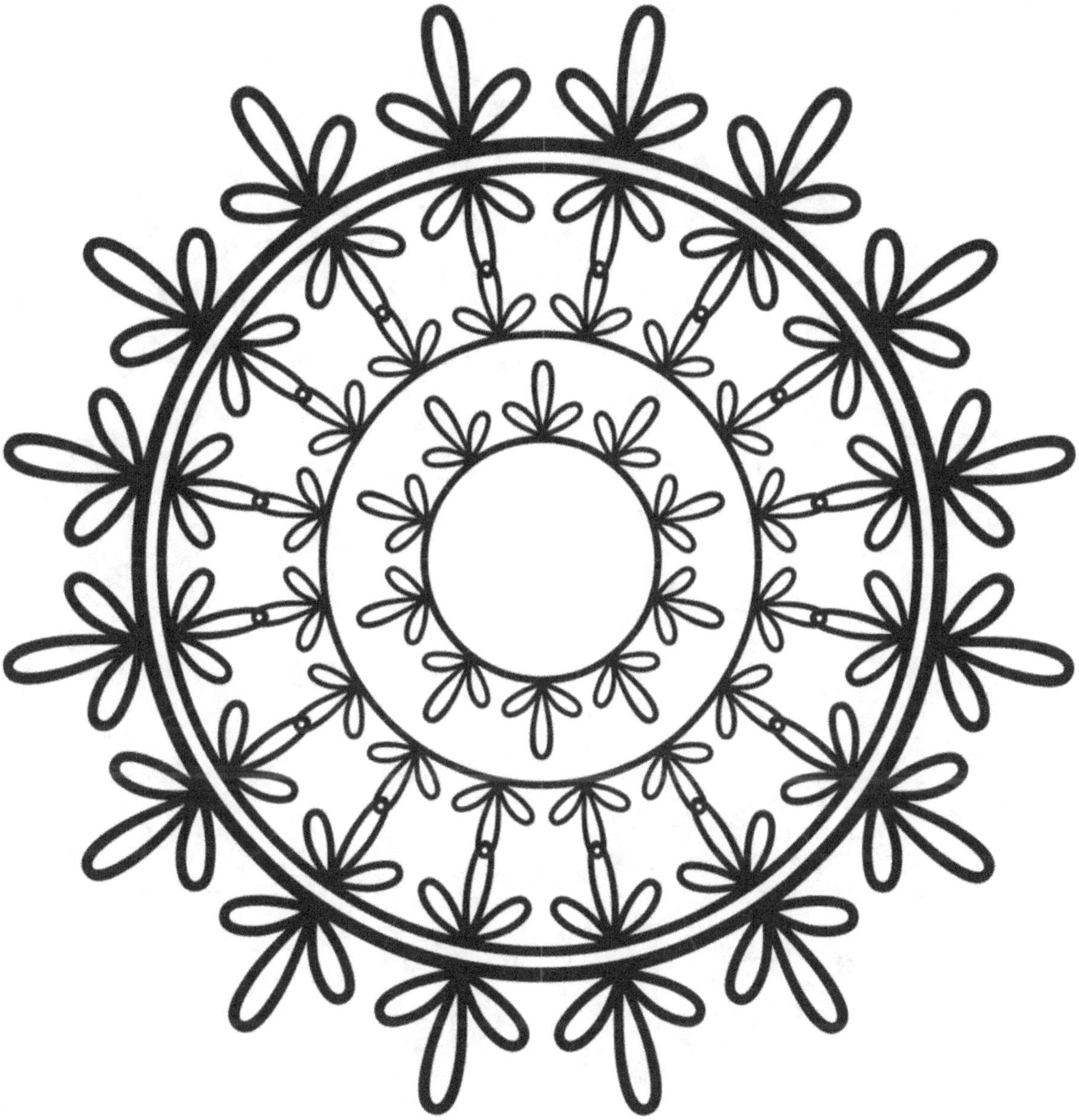

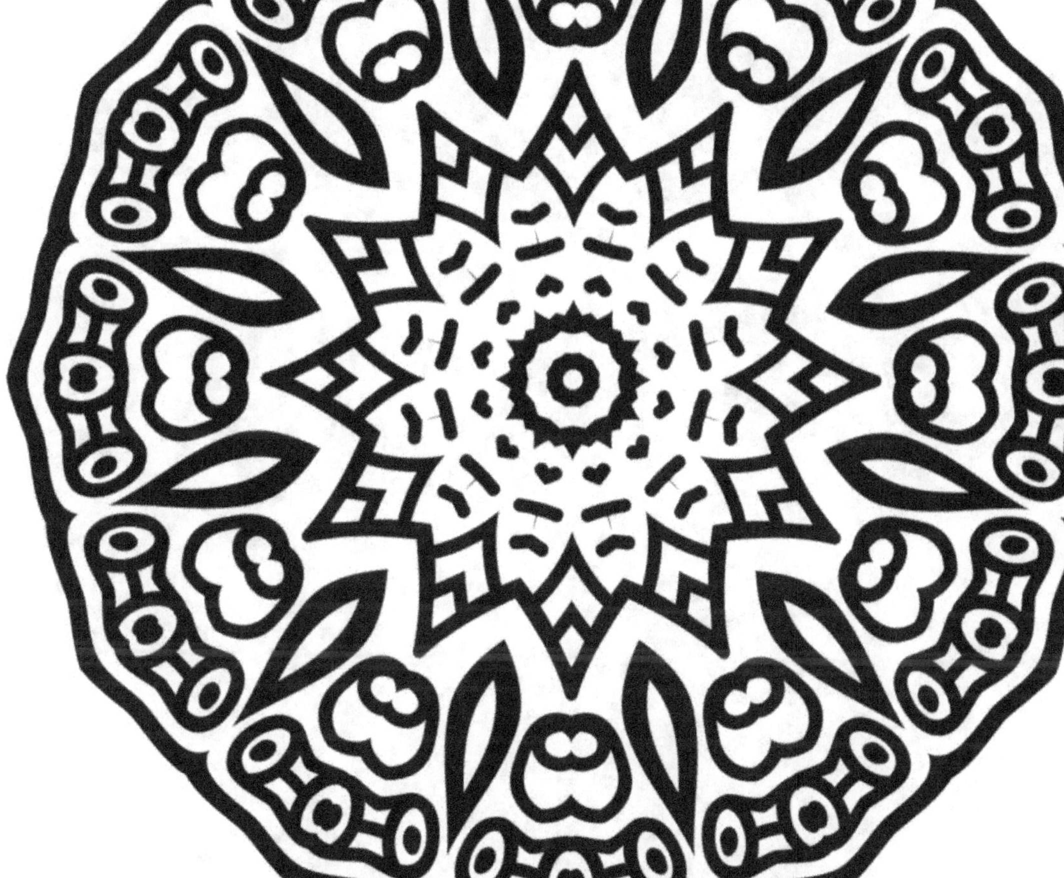

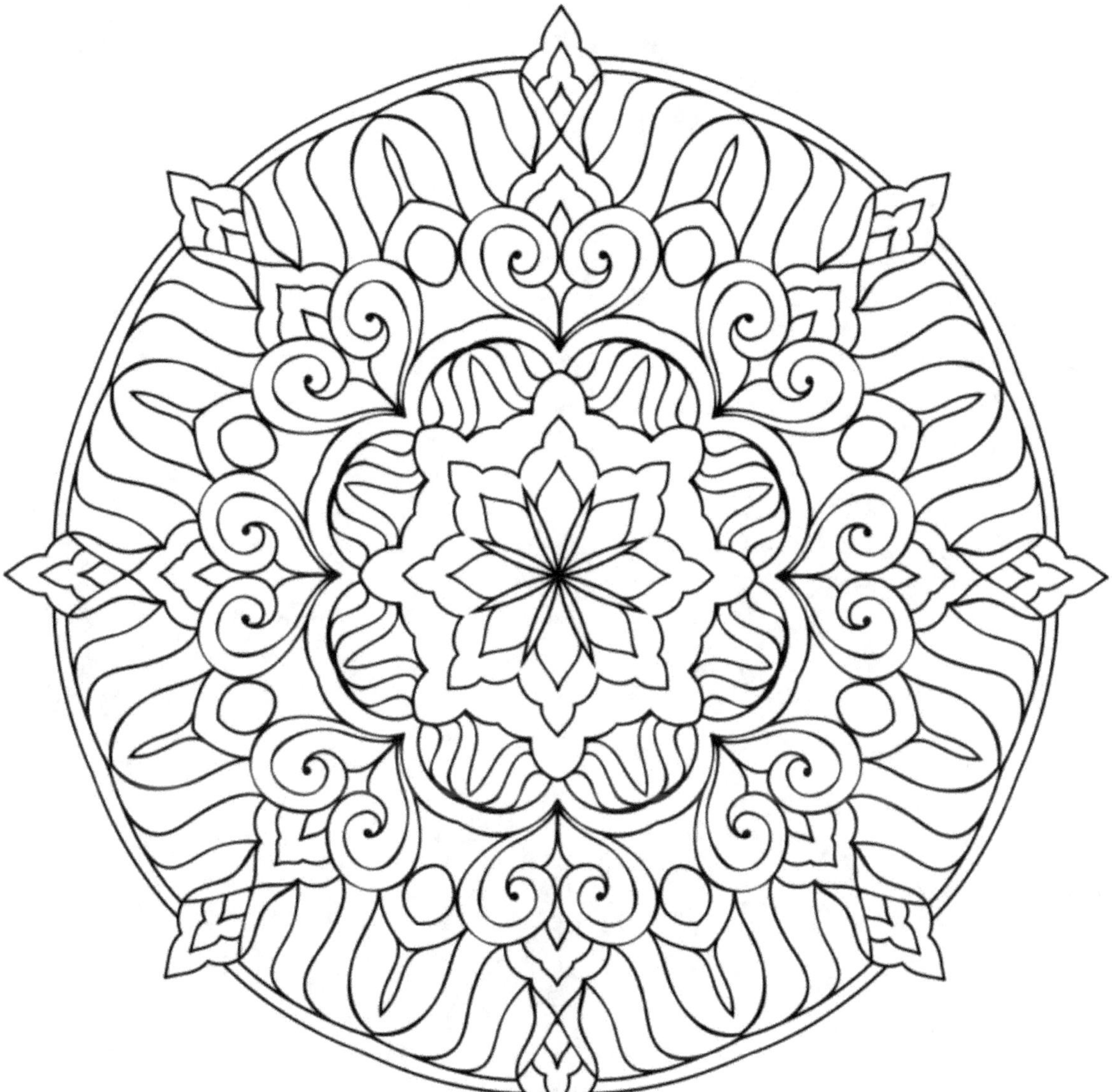

www.ingramcontent.com/pod-product-compliance
Lightning Source LLC
Chambersburg PA
CBHW080826180526
45168CB00006B/2594
9781515351016